Leyte Gulf 1944

The world's greatest sea battle

Leyte Gulf 1944

The world's greatest sea battle

Bernard Ireland · Illustrated by Howard Gerrard

First published in Great Britain in 2006 by Osprey Publishing, Midland House,
West Way, Botley, Oxford OX2 0PH, United Kindgom.
443 Park Avenue South, New York, NY 10016, USA
Email: info@ospreypublishing.com

A CIP catalogue record for this book is available from the British Library

ISBN: 978 1 84176 978 3

The author, Bernard Ireland, has asserted his right under the Copyright, Designs
and Patents Act, 1988, to be identified as the Author of this Work.
Typeset in Helvetica Neue and ITC New Baskerville
Design: The Black Spot
Maps by The Map Studio
3d bird's-eye views by The Black Spot
Battlescene artwork by Howard Gerrard
Index: Alan Thatcher
Originated by United Graphic, Singapore
Printed and bound in China through Worldprint

08 09 10 11 12   11 10 9 8 7 6 5 4

For a catalogue of all books published by Osprey please contact:

NORTH AMERICA
Osprey Direct, C/o Random House Distribution Center, 400 Hahn Road,
Westminster, MD 21157, USA
E-mail: info@ospreydirect.com

ALL OTHER REGIONS
Osprey Direct UK, P.O. Box 140, Wellingborough, Northants, NN8 2FA, UK
E-mail: info@ospreydirect.co.uk

www.ospreypublishing.com

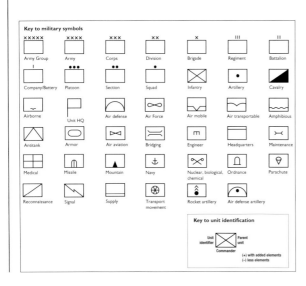

CONTENTS

THE PHILIPPINES AS AN OBJECTIVE

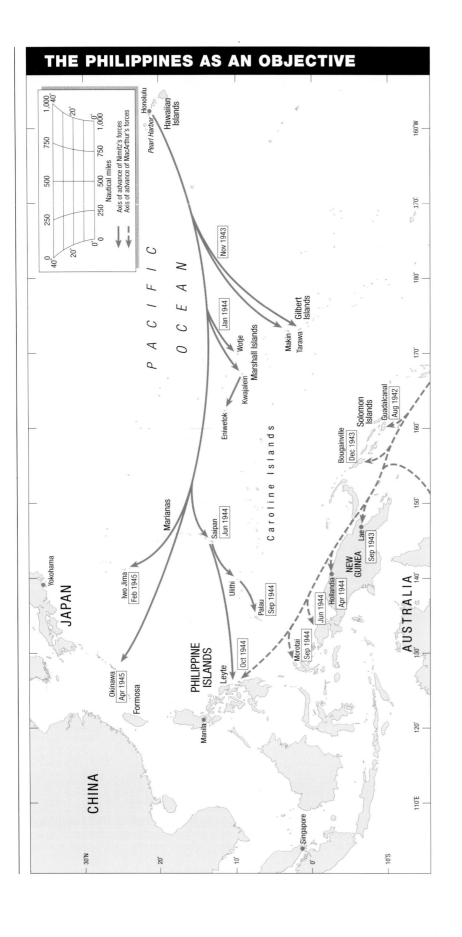

Nautical miles

Axis of advance of Nimitz's forces
Axis of advance of MacArthur's forces

PACIFIC OCEAN

Pearl Harbor
Honolulu
Hawaiian Islands

Nov 1943

Jan 1944

Wotje
Marshall Islands

Makin
Tarawa
Gilbert Islands

Eniwetok

Kwajalein

Caroline Islands

Marianas

Saipan
Jun 1944

Bougainville
Dec 1943

Solomon Islands
Guadalcanal
Aug 1942

Iwo Jima
Feb 1945

Ulithi

Palau
Sep 1944

Lae
Sep 1943

NEW GUINEA

Yokohama

JAPAN

Hollandia
Apr 1944

Jun 1944

Morotai
Sep 1944

Okinawa
Apr 1945

Formosa

PHILIPPINE ISLANDS

Leyte

Oct 1944

AUSTRALIA

Manila

CHINA

Singapore

INTRODUCTION

THE ROAD TO THE PHILIPPINES

On 6 May 1942, following a last-ditch resistance on Bataan and Corregidor, the Americans yielded control of the Philippine Islands to the Japanese, presenting the United States with a problem that had been foreseen by strategists from the time, back in 1898, when the territory had first become their responsibility.

The Pacific Ocean is vast. From the US west coast to Hawaii and the fleet base at Pearl Harbor is some 2,300 miles. From Hawaii to the Philippines is a further 4,800 miles. While the islands are thus about 7,000 miles from the United States, they are barely 1,500 miles from Japan.

Following her trouncing of Russia in 1904–05, Japan emerged as the major power of the western Pacific and a first class sea power in her own right. Her fleet was modelled on that of Great Britain, with whom she was in formal alliance. With Britain adopting a neutral or supportive stance, a militant and expansionist Japan was a prospect that alarmed American war planners, for outposts in the western Pacific – the Philippines, Guam and Wake Island – were vulnerable to Japanese seizure before America could act in their defence. Once occupied, they would be extremely difficult to recover in view of the distances involved.

Formal planning was thus initiated to evolve a strategy for the defence of these vulnerable dependencies. One of a number of contingency plans directed at foreign powers, that relevant to Japan was labelled Plan Orange. The plan was assisted by the completion, in 1914, of the Panama Canal which permitted the US Atlantic and Pacific Fleets to more rapidly reinforce each other.

By virtue of the 1902 Anglo-Japanese alliance, the latter power assisted the Allied cause during the First World War. This enabled it to occupy the vast western Pacific island groups – the Carolines, Marianas and Marshalls – that were German imperial holdings. At the peace, this occupation was extended to legal mandate.

A nonsensical naval race that developed after the war between the late Allies was halted by the Washington Conference of 1921–22. In an American political coup, the US Navy was enabled to equal the battle strength of the Royal Navy, while the Anglo-Japanese alliance was not renewed.

Japan was deeply slighted, both by the British defection and by the fact the conference failed to recognize her hard-won first-class naval status by permitting parity in battle fleets.

All too aware that 'the Mandates' lay astride the line of advance of any future American fleet charged with recovery of western Pacific possessions, the Americans ensured that articles of the ensuing Washington Treaty expressly forbade their further fortification or military exploitation. While it precluded converting Guam into an American Gibraltar, the treaty

Admiral King, Commander-in-Chief of the US Fleet and Chief of Naval Operations, King was an acerbic but highly professional officer who had overall direction of strategy in the Pacific. (NARA)

General Douglas MacArthur, President F.D. Roosevelt and Admiral Chester Nimitz at their meeting in Pearl Harbor where the decision to attack the Philippines was taken. (IWM EN335586)

specifically excluded Hawaii, signalling the emergence of Pearl Harbor as the major forward US fleet base.

Although the Japanese, in general, did respect the treaty terms, their innate secretiveness endlessly aroused American suspicions that they were building airfields on strategically important islands.

Thus assuming that any advancing battle fleet would have to fight its way westward opposed by a major enemy fleet supported by land-based air power, American planners made an organic air arm a priority. Aircraft carriers and naval aviation were thus prioritized from an early date. Because they had, in fact, observed the treaty ban on air bases, the Japanese identified a similar need and, like the Americans, developed carrier forces to the limits prescribed by agreement. Both fleets thus quickly became centred on their carriers, the destruction of which consequently became a matter of major concern.

Although United States policy was to deter Japanese adventurism in the western Pacific through a strong political and military stance, they continued to refine Plan Orange in tune with political realities and military capabilities. While not perfect, the plan proved to be remarkably prescient, providing the basis for the eventual American Pacific counter-offensive of 1942–45.

In essence, Plan Orange foresaw three phases. The first would see the Japanese overrunning American western Pacific possessions, which were accepted as indefensible in the face of a prolonged offensive. Phase Two would require the United States to acquire and develop suitable advance bases and to hold the line while strength was being built up. The final phase would be the endgame – blockade and strangulation of enemy supply routes, with deliberate advance to a point from which the enemy could be defeated by direct bombardment and invasion. The plan recognized that in this ocean-dominated theatre, sea supremacy would be of pivotal importance and that either side would seek to force a decisive naval engagement on its own terms.

In the event, Phase Two proved to be complex. Practical choice for axes of advance lay between an island-hopping thrust, westward across the Mandates, or a deliberate progress along the northern shore of New Guinea before heading north, probably via the Philippines. President Roosevelt favoured the naval-led former route, but was equally swayed by the eloquence of Gen Douglas MacArthur that the southern route, using Australia as a staging post, was superior. Controversially, both were adopted.

It has been observed that the two campaigns were analogous to those in Europe. The direct route to Japan herself, the central Pacific thrust commanded by Adm Chester Nimitz, was primary and comparable to the Allies' eastward advance from Normandy. That under MacArthur's leadership in the south was always secondary and could be compared with the Mediterranean campaign. Both pairs of campaigns were mutually supportive, confusing the enemy as to the next objective and obliging him to dissipate his strength. Only the enormous industrial capacity of the United States could sustain such a two-headed campaign. Even this was not infinite, however, and hard choices had to be made regarding which axis would see the next forward leap.

By the summer of 1944 Nimitz had secured the Marianas, while MacArthur controlled the whole length of New Guinea. A powerful argument now developed among the President and the Joint Chiefs of Staff. Nimitz favoured a bold move to take the Bonins or even Formosa, both to bring the Japanese home islands within bombardment range of B-29s and to cut the enemy's supply route to the south. MacArthur argued emotionally and strongly for the Philippines, strategically the commencement of a long left hook. Beyond this, the general insisted that the United States had a moral obligation to undertake the early liberation of 16 million loyal Filipinos. With an eye to post-war trade, it was also pointed out that it would put the Americans in a favourable light.

Nimitz's men argued that the Philippines archipelago comprises 7,000 islands and stretches some 750 miles from north to south. It was illogical to argue that it was possible to liberate anything like the whole population, while a campaign in the islands would soak up vast resources for considerable periods. None the less, powerful sentiment proved persuasive. The Philippines would be next.

CHRONOLOGY

20 September–18 October Adm Halsey's Third Fleet carrier aircraft eliminate bulk of Japanese air power in Northern Philippines.

10–15 October Adm Kinkaid's Seventh Fleet sails from Manus, Hollandia, etc., with US Sixth Army to commence recovery of Philippines by amphibious landing in Leyte Gulf.

17 October Preliminary US activities alert Japanese. Adm Toyoda activates SHO-1 counterplan.

18 October (0100) V Adm Kurita, with First Striking Force, leaves Lingga Roads (near Singapore).

19 October Halsey's Third Fleet including V Adm Mitscher's carrier force (TF38) positioned to east of Philippines. (TF38 comprises four task groups: TG 38.1, TG 38.2, TG 38.3 and TG 38.4.)

20 October (1000) Leyte Gulf landing commences.

(p.m.) Kurita's First Striking Force arrives at Brunei Bay.

(evening) V Adm Ozawa's Northern Force sails from Japan.

21 October First Striking Force divided into Centre Group (Kurita) and Southern Force (V Adm Nishimura).

22 October (0800) Kurita's Centre Group departs Brunei Bay.

(a.m.) V Adm Shima's Second Striking Force departs Japan.

(1500) Nishimura's Southern Force departs Brunei Bay.

(p.m.) Halsey detaches TG 38.1 and TG 38.4 to Ulithi for re-supply.

23 October (0630) Kurita's Centre Group attacked by US submarines in Palawan Passage.

(a.m.) Halsey recalls TG 38.4.

(a.m.) Kurita's Centre Group enters Sibuyan Sea.

24 October (0030) Kurita's Centre Group reported off Mindoro.

(0830) Halsey recalls TG 38.1.

(0905) Nishimura's Southern Force reported in Sulu Sea.

Battle of Sibuyan Sea – Kurita's Centre Group attacked by TG 38.2 and TG 38.4 aircraft at 1025, 1245, 1330, 1415 and 1550. (Damage inflicted greatly over-reported by US aviators.)

(1155) Shima's Second Striking Force reported off Cagayan Islands.

(p.m.) Kinkaid anticipates that Nishimura and Shima are heading for Leyte Gulf via Surigao Strait and orders suitable dispositions by Seventh Fleet.

(1530) Kurita's Centre Group (without air cover and under heavy air attack) reverses course.

(1540) Ozawa's Northern Force sighted by TG 38.4 aircraft.

(1715) Kurita's Centre Group resumes original course.

(1735) Kurita's Centre Group reported by night-flying TG 38.2 aircraft (Halsey none the less considers Kurita no longer a major threat and resolves to destroy Ozawa's carriers).

(2022) Halsey's Third Fleet heads north after Ozawa. (Kinkaid assumes Halsey has left rearguard. He has not.)

(2115) Kurita's Centre Group reported steering for San Bernardino Strait.

(2300) Nishimura's Southern Force attacked by PT boats near Bohol.

(2315) Halsey concentrated night-fliers to locate Ozawa. Kurita no longer tracked.

25 October (0001) Shima's Second Striking Force is trailing Nishimura's Southern Force by 40 miles but not in communication.

(0015) Nishimura's Southern Force is attacked by PT boats off Panaon. Further attacks at 0140 and 0205.

(0030) Kurita's Centre Group exits San Bernardino Strait unopposed.

25 October (0200–0400) Nishimura's Southern Force under destroyer attack in Surigao Strait.

(0325) Shima's Second Striking Force under PT boat attack.

(0350–0410) Battle of Surigao Strait/Nishimura's Southern Force destroyed by R Adm Oldendorf's Seventh Fleet battleships.

(0425) Shima's Second Striking Force withdraws without engaging Oldendorf.

(0645) Halsey informed of Surigao Strait action. Kinkaid learns that San Bernardino Strait is unguarded.

(0648) Kurita's Centre Group sights R Adm C. Sprague's TG 77.4 escort carrier group off Samar.

(0700–0910) Battle off Samar. Desperate defence by CVEs and escort blocks Kurita short of Leyte Gulf.

(0740) Sprague's TG 77.4 sustains first deliberate Kamikaze attacks.

(0800–1800) Battle of Cape Engaño. Ozawa's Northern Force loses all its carriers to attacks by Halsey's Third Fleet TG 38.3 and TG 38.4 aircraft.

(0822) Halsey learns that Kurita is attacking Sprague, with assistance from Oldendorf three hours distant.

(0848) Halsey orders TG 38.1 to Sprague's assistance, although this is also three hours distant.

(0910) Kurita's Centre Group breaks off action but remains in area.

(1000) Aware of Kinkaid's desperate calls for assistance, Fleet Adm Nimitz queries Halsey as to his whereabouts.

(1055) Halsey combines TG 38.2 with the bulk of the Third Fleet battleship force to form new group, TG 34.5. (Even at full speed, TG 34.5 is still 14 hours from San Bernardino.)

(1310) Kurita's Centre Group abandons attempts to reach Leyte Gulf and begins retirement.

(2140) Kurita's Centre Group retreats through San Bernardino.

26 October (0100) TG 34.5 arrives at San Bernardino and abandons pursuit.

(0810) Kurita's Centre Group sighted in Tablas Strait.

(a.m.–p.m.) Kurita's Centre Group attacked by TG 38.1 and TG 38.2 aircraft and US Army bombers.

(p.m.) Halsey's Third Fleet carrier force (TG 38) resumes cover of Leyte Gulf.

The battleship _Haruna_, which was present in the battle off Samar, is bombed by aircraft of Task Force 38 at a mooring near Kure, Japan. She was eventually sunk. (NARA)

OPPOSING COMMANDERS

US COMMANDERS

Strategic control of the Third Fleet was exercised by **Admiral Chester W. Nimitz** who, based at Pearl Harbor, vested tactical control in Adm William F. Halsey. In both character and manner the two men contrasted considerably. Nimitz had sure strategic sense, never rushing to a decision. With subordinates he was invariably calm and courteous, his officers trusting his judgement implicitly. When Allied forces in the Pacific were still on the back foot, morale was low and mistakes were made. Nimitz acknowledged that such failings were inevitable and was always prepared to offer an individual a second chance. A man of rare gifts, he commanded the US Pacific Fleet from December 1941 until December 1945.

Where Nimitz was the supreme administrator, **Admiral William F. Halsey** was the archetypal salt horse. First a destroyer man, an area in which he was an authority, he moved on to carrier operations. No great thinker, his major characteristic was a pronounced tendency to aggression, offset by a popular touch that endeared him to subordinates and public alike. The popular press, needing a hero, saddled him with the soubriquet 'Bull' Halsey. He began to live up to it, his natural

Vice-Admiral Marc A. Mitscher, USN (Com-fast carrier forces), and Fleet-Admiral Chester W. Nimitz, USN (Cincpac-POA) are shown on board a US ship off Guam, 1945. (Naval Historical Center)

aggression leading to impetuosity. When someone with Halsey's responsibilities made mistakes, they tended to be big ones, and his later career progressed mainly through Nimitz' tolerance and his own status as a national icon.

Vice Admiral Marc A. Mitscher, in tactical command of the fast carrier force (TF38), was a career naval aviator, one of the first such to qualify. Nominally Halsey's deputy, Mitscher was endlessly bypassed by his Admiral. His appointment by Nimitz had been controversial but sound. In 1944 he was 57 years of age but, wizened and of slight stature, looked older. Commencing in March 1944, his post made heavy demands on him. In July 1945, as the final battle for Japan was shaping up, he was posted ashore but died, still in harness, just 19 months later.

General Douglas MacArthur was officially Supreme Commander of the Southwest Pacific Area, but referred to himself as 'Commander-in-Chief'. His family had strong ties with the Philippines and their people, and the Japanese occupation had initiated in him something of a personal crusade for their deliverance. He was a man of great 'presence', his eloquence and force of character greatly influencing the choice of the islands as the next objective on the road to Japan.

MacArthur liked to dress unconventionally, often to be seen in various combinations of brogues, army-issue trousers, leather Air Force jacket and Philippine general's hat. His mode of command was also not quite 'per book' but no one doubted who was in charge.

Despite having a senior subordinate commander for each of the three major services, MacArthur ran a staff along army lines, the other service representatives acting as technical consultants. Clear as to his objectives, the general was equally clear in his stated intentions. All operations were set up by himself, his subordinate commanders first being issued with a set of 'Warning Instructions' which defined their tasks in broad terms. Having given them time to digest these, he would call them together for a conference at his headquarters. Following a thorough discussion and analysis, MacArthur then produced their 'Operation Instructions', executive orders for the next phase of detailed planning. These were always cited as models of clarity and brevity. From this point, he made it his practice not to interfere with his subordinates' tasks.

Vice-Admiral Thomas C. Kinkaid had commanded the Seventh Fleet since November 1942. Well-trusted by MacArthur, he had twice been transferred by him to relieve existing commanders. Although once described as 'a noisy Irishman who loves a rough-house', Kinkaid comes across as patient and thorough, and it was his attention to detail that was to prove so important in coming events. He was a gunnery specialist who had seen most time in capital ships.

Rear-Admiral Jesse B. Oldendorf was a good example of the thoroughly reliable career officer who could always be relied upon to do the right thing yet who lacked the vital ingredient essential for higher command. Commanding the bombardment groups at Leyte Gulf, he would be called upon to switch from the routine of gunfire support to the fighting of a critically important surface action. In this, his rapid planning proved to be meticulous, although, interestingly, he appointed subordinate officers to the major roles, for which he gave full credit. Ultimately, having crushed his opponent, he lacked the killer instinct.

Vice-Admiral Marc A. Mitscher: Quietly spoken and slight in figure, Mitscher generated a loyal following through his sincere concern for the men under his command as well as for his fighting qualities. (NARA)

Vice-Admiral Thomas C. Kinkaid watching landings at Leyte from the bridge of his flagship USS *Wasatch*. As Commander 7th Fleet, Kinkaid directed US naval forces at Leyte and throughout the Philippines. (NARA)

V Admiral Kurita commanded the Centre Group, which incorporated two of the most powerful battleships ever built, *Yamato* and *Musashi*. (NARA)

JAPANESE COMMANDERS

Admiral Toyoda Soemu, Chief of the Naval General Staff, was one of a group of influential naval officers who were convinced from the outset that Japan could never prevail in the face of American industrial might. He was, none the less, an excellent strategist and one-time candidate for the post of Navy Minister. His career had suffered through his poor relationship with the all-powerful army lobby, his critics describing him detrimentally as being 'too talkative [and with] a strong tendency to be disruptive'.

Vice-Admiral Ozawa Jisaburo, in contrast, worked well with the army but showed little interest in his personal advancement, later refusing promotion to full admiral. Known as a first-class fighting admiral, he was an able tactician and had specialized in torpedoes and night-fighting. Taller than average, he had a forbidding appearance, but got the best out of his subordinates, by whom he was well respected.

Vice-Admiral Kurita Takeo was never regarded as one of the navy's intellectuals and had never attended War College. He was happier in a sea command and had always impressed in exercises and in war-gaming. Perceived as reserved by nature, he was always pleasant and cheerful. He, too, was a specialist in torpedo warfare.

Vice-Admiral Nishimura Shojo was rated more highly than Kurita by the experienced Ozawa. Like Kurita, he was an able sea officer and a torpedo specialist. He was regarded as being 'too nice a person', avoiding heated argument and being too easily persuaded by others.

OPPOSING FORCES

US NAVAL FORCES IN THE WESTERN PACIFIC

As far as operations in the Pacific were concerned, all allied ships involved belonged to, or were controlled by, either the US Third or Seventh Fleet. The Third Fleet was part of Adm Nimitz' command, its flag officer being Adm William F. Halsey. Its overall remit was to 'cover and support' the Leyte expansion. The Seventh Fleet came under Gen MacArthur, and was commanded by V Adm Thomas C. Kinkaid. Its task was to 'transport, establish and support forces ashore in the Leyte area'.

Third Fleet

The Third Fleet consisted almost entirely of Task Force 38 (TF38), which was organized in four fast carrier task groups (TG). The primary command structure took the form below:

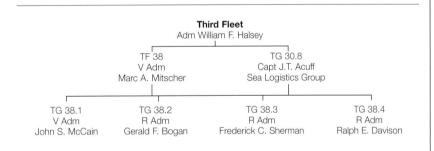

In all, TF 38 comprised about 90 ships, fairly evenly disposed between the four task groups. Each task group was, as far as possible, a self-contained combat unit, capable of undertaking independent missions. Each contained, typically, two attack carriers (CV), two light carriers (CVL), one or more battleships (BB), up to four cruisers (a mix of heavy (CA), light (CL) and anti-craft (CL(AA))), and a destroyer squadron, usually of 16 destroyers (DD) organized in four divisions.

Essential to the Third Fleet's ability to keep the sea for extended periods was its Sea Logistics Group (TG 30.8), which answered to Halsey rather than Mitscher. Its size was impressive, including over 30 fleet oilers (AO), of which half were on call at any time. To meet the high attrition rates of TF38's carriers there were also 11 escort carriers (CVE) carrying replacement aircraft. A dozen dedicated ammunition ships (AE) were organized in two echelons. Finally, there were ten salvage tugs (AT) to assist the survival of battle-damaged ships.

US Navy carriers at Ulithi Atoll: front to back USS *Wasp*, USS *Yorktown*, USS *Hornet*, USS *Hancock*, USS *Ticonderoga*, USS *Lexington*. (NARA)

An armada of American ships steaming along the coast of Leyte Island. The American investment in the campaign almost guaranteed success. (NARA)

This large and valuable fleet train had its own escort screen, comprising 18 destroyers and 26 destroyer escorts (DE).

The Sea Logistics task group was, itself, divided into four task units (TU 30.8.1 to TU 30.8.4), one of which was assigned to each of TF38's task groups. Replenishment-at-sea (RAS) was conducted to such a high standard that all 90-odd ships of TF 38 could refuel and re-store within one daylight period. During the Leyte Gulf operation, the Third Fleet was at sea for 13 weeks out of 16.

At the 'sharp end' of the Third Fleet were its carriers. Excepting the 1938-built *Enterprise*, all attack carriers were of the new 33,400-ton Essex-class. Light carriers were all of the new 14,200-ton Independence class, converted from heavy cruiser hulls and capable of over 31 knots.

An Essex carried an air group typically comprising 40–45 fighters (F6F Hellcats), 25–35 dive bombers (SB2C Helldivers) and 18 torpedo bombers (TBF/TBM Avengers). A CVL, on the other hand, would typically carry a smaller wing of 25 fighters and nine torpedo bombers.

The carriers were also the primary enemy targets, the greatest threat to them airborne. Battleships thus commonly acted as anti-aircraft escorts, steaming close aboard the carriers. As we shall see, however, they could rapidly be deployed as the heavy component of a surface action group.

Seventh Fleet
Very much subordinated to the Army and geared to assist in its amphibious, hopping progress along the 1,500-mile northern coastline of New Guinea, the Seventh Fleet was considered a 'brown water' navy. Headed by a handful of cruisers and destroyers, it comprised mainly amphibious craft, minor combatants and, incongruously, submarines. The command structure thus looked like this:

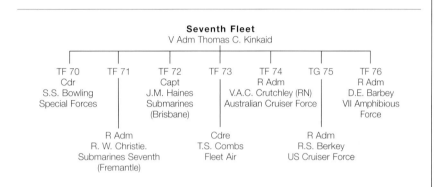

In addition, there was the Service Force, Seventh Fleet (Cdre R.G. Coman), which handled logistics. This force bore no TF or TG label.

As constituted above, Kinkaid's command was manifestly unsuitable and inadequate for mounting the planned assault on the Philippines. Adm Nimitz therefore temporarily transferred from the Pacific Fleet what was virtually a fleet in itself. These temporary additions were organized as three further task forces, namely TF77, 78 and 79.

The stem structure for the Leyte operation was thus as below:

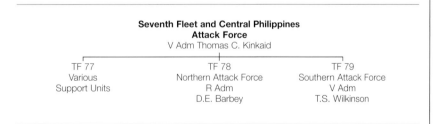

As elements of these task forces were involved in major naval actions as well as the landings, it is useful to note their composition. The tally TF77 was used by Kinkaid to identify any special attack force and, during the Leyte operation, it had no overall commander but comprised several task groups and task units. Most important of these was TG 77.4, the escort carrier force which, commanded by R Adm Thomas L. Sprague, was charged with providing air support over the assault area. Including 16 small carriers (CVE), it was organized in three task units.

A Grumman Avenger stands ready for launch on a US carrier while a destroyer follows in its wake. (NARA)

Escort Carrier Group TG 77.4 R Adm Thomas L. Sprague		
TU 77.4.1 R Adm Thomas L. Sprague Four CVE Three DD Four DE	TU 77.4.2 R Adm Felix B. Stump Two CVE	TU 77.4.3 R Adm Clifton A.F. Sprague Four CVE
	R Adm W.D. Sample Four CVE Three DD Four DE	R Adm R.A. Ofstie Two CVE Three DD Four DE

The cruiser forces TF74 and TF75 were now combined under R Adm Berkey as TG 77.3. Minesweeping and hydrographic details were the responsibility of TG 77.5, and beach demolition TG 77.6.

It was the business of task forces TF78 (R Adm Daniel E. Barbey) and TF79 (V Adm Theodore S. Wilkinson) to transport and land the military forces in the northern and southern sectors respectively, and it was their landing that triggered the naval actions that are the subject of this monograph. Of direct relevance are the support forces attached to each.

Accompanying Wilkinson's TF79 was Fire Support Unit South (R Adm Jesse B. Oldendorf). Intended for shore bombardment details, this force included three veteran battleships (*Tennessee, California* and *Pennsylvania*), three heavy and three light cruisers, and 13 destroyers.

A similar force, Fire Support Unit North (R Adm George L. Weyler) was attached to TF78. Its three elderly capital ships (*Mississippi, Maryland* and *West Virginia*) were, however, supported by only three destroyers, three more having to be borrowed from Oldendorf.

The availability of these forces was to be of crucial importance.

USS *Essex* underway, carrying SBD scout bombers, F6F fighters and TBF/TBM torpedo planes. *Essex* gave its name to the new 33,400-ton attack carrier class that made up the majority of heavy carriers in the Third Fleet. (NARA)

JAPANESE NAVAL FORCES

Following the Battle of the Philippine Sea ('The Great Marianas Turkey Shoot') of June 1944, the Imperial Japanese Navy was a service in dire trouble. Over 400 aircraft had been lost during the two-day action, with probably 450 aircrew. As there were no replacement air wings, the carrier force had been reduced to negligible offensive potential until such times as an emergency training programme produced further aircrew. At the time of the Leyte operation, these were still awaited, their training slowed, indeed truncated, by lack of aviation fuel.

Shortage of bunker fuel was also causing the fleet major problems. Supplies had to be freighted mainly from Borneo, some 2,500 miles distant over seas now infested with American submarines. These particularly targeted tankers, a strategy so successful that the bulk of the Japanese fleet had to be relocated to a point closer to fuel sources.

In July 1944 Adm Oikawa, head of the Navy Department at the Imperial Headquarters, informed Adm Toyoda, Commanders-in-Chief of what was termed the Combined Fleet, that its main strength would move to Lingga Roads, some 90 miles south-east of Singapore. The carrier force and its supporting ships were to remain in the Inland Sea until replacement aircrew were trained to an acceptable standard. A few units remained in northern Honshu and the Philippines.

Vice-Admiral Mikawa commanded the Second South Sea Fleet and the South West Area Force in the Philippines. (NARA)

Although such fragmentation was a severe encumbrance to rapid reaction, the fleet was still not released from its obligation to seek a decisive battle. This desire for a Trafalgar-style action was inherited from the British Royal Navy when it acted as mentor, and called for an all-out trial of strength to decide sea supremacy. It was a doctrine that appealed to the Japanese but, for the first year or so of the Pacific war, when they enjoyed numerical superiority, they were unable to pin down the Americans.

By the autumn of 1944, however, the picture had changed drastically. The US Navy had mushroomed while that of the Japanese had been greatly reduced by attrition. Aircraft carriers had emerged as queens of the board and air superiority had become essential, not only for victory but also for sheer survival. In carrier operations, the Americans excelled. They had more and better ships, new types of aircraft and an aircrew training programme that guaranteed a steady flow of replacements.

In view of its new dispositions and the current necessity of operating under a protective umbrella of shore-based aircraft, the best area that the Japanese fleet could hope to defend was one bounded by a line from Japan to the Ryukyus, thence to Formosa and the Philippines, and along the Malay barrier.

To counter an assault on various points of this periphery, the Japanese developed four so-called SHO plans. A key feature of each of these plans was effective integration between naval forces and land-based air power.

Although reduced by nearly three years of war, the Japanese fleet remained formidable. It could still muster seven battleships, 11 carriers, 13 heavy and seven light cruisers. Destroyers, so essential to any operation, had been reduced by profligate expenditure from 151 to just 63, while only 49 submarines remained.

Superficial comparison with Halsey's Third Fleet might lead to an assumption that a 'decisive battle' was not out of the question, for the

American admirals, strength stood at seven battleships, eight attack and eight light carriers, eight heavy and nine light cruisers. Halsey, however, was concentrated where his opponents were not. Halsey's ships were all modern, all well-trained and could, to an extent, be replaced. He also had Kinkaid's Seventh Fleet as back-up.

Japanese ships were of varying vintage and their radar and communications much inferior to those of the Americans (although, as events were to show, equipment is only as good as those using it). The crucial factor, however, was that between them, the Third Fleet's carriers could muster 800 or more aircraft.

The Japanese were also addicted to complexity. Although meticulously detailed, their operational plans were over-complicated and, as with their plans, so with their command organization. Subsequent to the recent cabinet re-shuffle, this looked like:

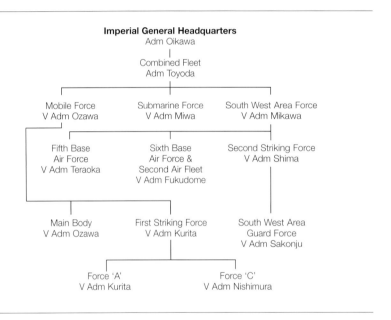

The actual composition of the forces relevant to the Leyte Gulf battles was as follows:

(i)   Main Body (Ozawa). One fleet and three light carriers, mustering a total of about 120 aircraft. Two hybrid battleship/carriers. Three light cruisers, eight destroyers, six smaller, two tankers. To simplify the narrative, this will be called the Northern Force.

(ii)   Force 'A' (Kurita). Five battleships/battle cruisers. Ten heavy and two light cruisers, 15 destroyers. This will be called the Centre Group.

(iii) Force 'C' (Nishimura). Two battleships. One heavy cruiser and four destroyers. This will be called the Van of the Southern Force.

(iv)   Second Striking Force (Shima). One heavy and one light cruiser, seven destroyers. This will be called the Rear of the Southern Force.

South West Area Guard Force (Sakonju). This group was engaged in staging a diversionary landing. It played no part in the main actions and its activities have, therefore, been omitted.

JAPANESE LAND-BASED AIR POWER IN THE PHILIPPINES

Japanese air forces based on Philippine airfields were also subject to a complex command structure. Before the loss of Saipan in July 1944 brought home the seriousness of the war, the Japanese Army Air Force played no part in naval operations. By the end of that month, however, agreement had been reached that the Army would, in normal circumstances, control operations over the Philippines but that the Navy would take over should the activity move predominantly offshore. All long-range patrols and searches would be undertaken by the Navy, which service would share responsibility for shorter range details. There existed considerable friction between the services, and such divided responsibilities could only cause further problems.

Naval land-based air was organized in so-called 'Base Air Forces' of which the Fifth and Sixth appear in the command structure above. Army air was formed into 'Air Armies', whose areas of responsibility could overlap those of the naval Base Air Forces. There also existed joint command, as with V Adm Teraoka's Fifth Base Air Force and LtGen Tominaga's Fourth Air Arm, which jointly covered the Philippines. Teraoka was replaced by V Adm Onishi on 20 October.

A US raid on Rabaul harbour, New Britain, as part of the prelude to the US campaign in the Philippines. (Associated Press © EMPICS)

V Adm Fukudome's Sixth Base Air Force covered the important neighbouring area, including the southern Japanese island of Kyushu, Formosa and the chain of Ryukyu Islands that linked them. These formed both an effective route to Japan as well as a convenient route south for aerial reinforcements for the Philippines.

Between them, the two services operated about 270 airfields and seaplane stations throughout the islands, including a dozen on Leyte itself. Little more than a quarter were all-weather installations, however, while the advantages of dispersal were offset by the organization being hammered and fragmented by repeated air strikes from Mitscher's Third Fleet carriers.

Such action was the usual preliminary to a major Allied assault and, again, alerted the Japanese to an impending move. The operations were unusually thorough, however, with China-based American bombers hitting Formosa and Hong Kong while others from Morotai, west of New Guinea and at the very limit of MacArthur's advance to date, raided airfields on Mindanao and outlying garrisons in Truk and the Carolines.

It was over Formosa itself, however, that TF38 expended its greatest effort, unleashing nearly 1,400 sorties on the island during 12–15 October. Besides a claimed 40 merchant ships, over 500 aircraft were lost to the Japanese.

By 20 October, the date of the Leyte landings, hardly 100 Japanese aircraft were estimated to remain operational in the Philippines. Fukudome was ordered to fly in every aircraft that remained to him on Formosa. Within two days the number had doubled, with an estimated 180 arriving within a week.

Land-based Japanese air power was, in fact, quickly augmented in the islands, but too late to have any bearing on the course of the great naval actions. Sparse and fragmented, it was incapable of inflicting decisive damage to the invader and a vital element of the Japanese defence plan had effectively ceased to function.

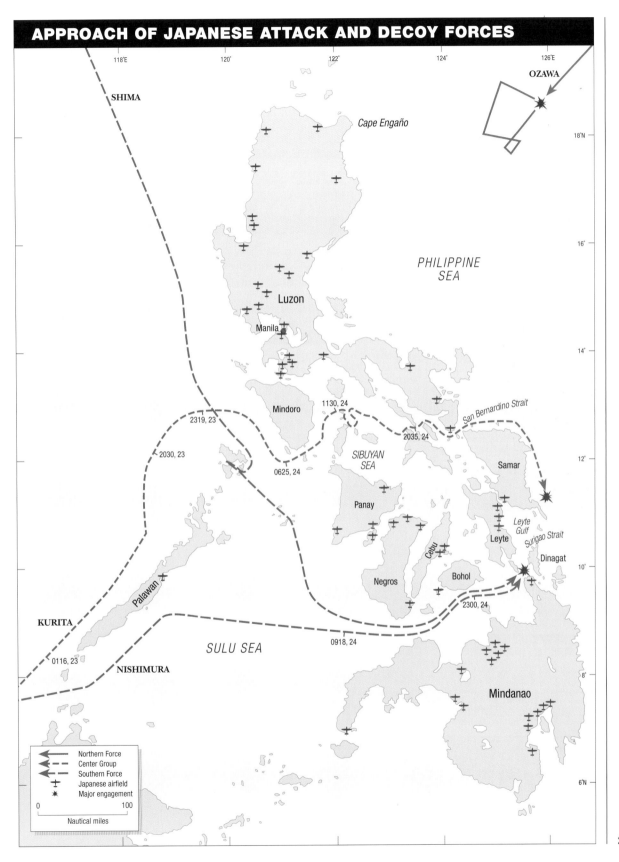

118°E   120°   122°   124°   126°E

OZAWA

SHIMA

Cape Engaño

18°N

16°

PHILIPPINE SEA

Luzon

Manila

14°

Mindoro

2319, 23   1130, 24

2030, 23   *SIBUYAN SEA*   2035, 24   San Bernardino Strait

0625, 24   12°

Samar

Panay   *Leyte Gulf*   Surigao Strait

Cebu   Leyte

Dinagat

Negros   Bohol   10°

KURITA   Palawan   2300, 24

SULU SEA   0918, 24

0116, 23   Mindanao

NISHIMURA   8°

Northern Force
Center Group
Southern Force
Japanese airfield
Major engagement

0   100

Nautical miles

6°N

OPPOSING STRATEGIES

US OPERATIONAL COMMAND STRUCTURE AND PLAN

The scale of the landings in Leyte Gulf was such that two beaches were involved. Designated Northern and Southern, each was about three miles in length, the two being separated by about 11 miles. There were, in consequence, two attack forces, also designated Northern and Southern, and leading to the following command structure:

Supreme Commander, Southwest Pacific Area
Gen Douglas MacArthur

Commander Central Philippines Attack Force
V Adm Thomas C. Kinkaid
(Embarked: LtGen Walter Krueger, Commander Expeditionary Force)

Northern Attack Force	Southern Attack Force
R Adm Daniel E. Barbey	V Adm Theodore S. Wilkinson
Embarked: X Corps	Embarked: XXIV Corps
(MajGen Franklin C. Sibert)	(MajGen J.R. Hodge)

General Douglas MacArthur wades ashore at Leyte. This for MacArthur was the vindication of a personal crusade and commitment to the people of the Philippines. (NARA)

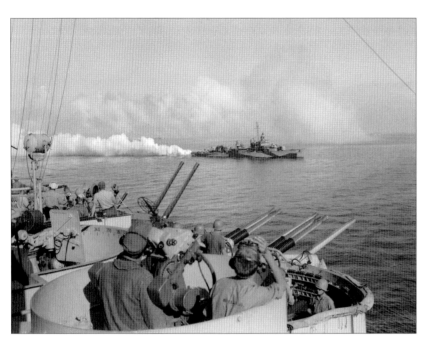

In accordance with standard procedure, V Adm Kinkaid commanded all personnel until the army contingents were established ashore, at which time their command transferred to LtGen Krueger.

To Kinkaid's Seventh Fleet MacArthur assigned the following tasks:

(i)   To transport and establish landing forces ashore in the Leyte Gulf–Surigao Strait area, as arranged with the Commanding General, Sixth US Army (i.e. Krueger), and

(ii) To support the operation by:

    (a) Providing air protection for convoys and direct air support for the landing and subsequent operations, including anti-submarine patrol of the Gulf and combat air patrol over the amphibious ships and craft, from his escort carriers (CVE);

    (b) Lifting reinforcements and supplies to Leyte in naval assault shipping;

    (c) Preventing Japanese reinforcement by sea of its Leyte garrisons;

    (d) Opening Surigao Strait for Allied use, and sending naval forces into Visayan (central Philippine) waters to support current and future operations, and

    (e) Providing submarine reconnaissance, lifeguard service and escort-of-convoy.

As detailed earlier, the Seventh Fleet and its logistics services had needed to be substantially augmented from US Pacific Fleet resources in order to fulfil these tasks.

Entirely independent of these forces, and under the control of Adm Nimitz was Adm Halsey's Third Fleet. Charged with 'covering and supporting [Southwest Pacific Forces] in order to assist in the seizure and occupation of all objectives in the Central Philippines' its overall brief was necessarily wider and less specific than Kinkaid's.

To ensure that orders to the two fleets were complementary, they were drafted by MacArthur's operations officer and Nimitz' plans officer working together.

Specifically, Third Fleet's cover and support for the landings comprised:

(i) Striking Okinawa, Formosa and Northern Leyte on 10–13 October;
(ii) Striking the Bicol peninsula, Leyte, Cebu and Negros, and supporting the landings on Leyte on 16–20 October, and
(iii) Operating strategic support of the Leyte operation, by destroying enemy naval and air forces threatening the Philippines area, on and after 21 October.

Cruiser USS *Nashville*, the flagship of Gen Douglas MacArthur, anchored off Leyte during the landings of 21 October 1944. *Nashville* provided fire support for the landings. (NARA)

LCTs stand off the beaches of Leyte while troops wade ashore. Bombardments from battleships and cruisers darken the sky. (Associated Press © EMPICS)

The major purpose of the landings, as envisaged by the Joint Chiefs of Staff (JCS) was effectively to separate Japanese forces based in the major islands of Luzon in the north and Mindanao in the south. This would permit the establishment of a springboard from which the strategically essential island of Luzon could be taken, while containing and by-passing the non-essential territory of Mindanao.

LEYTE: ASSAULT ORGANIZATION

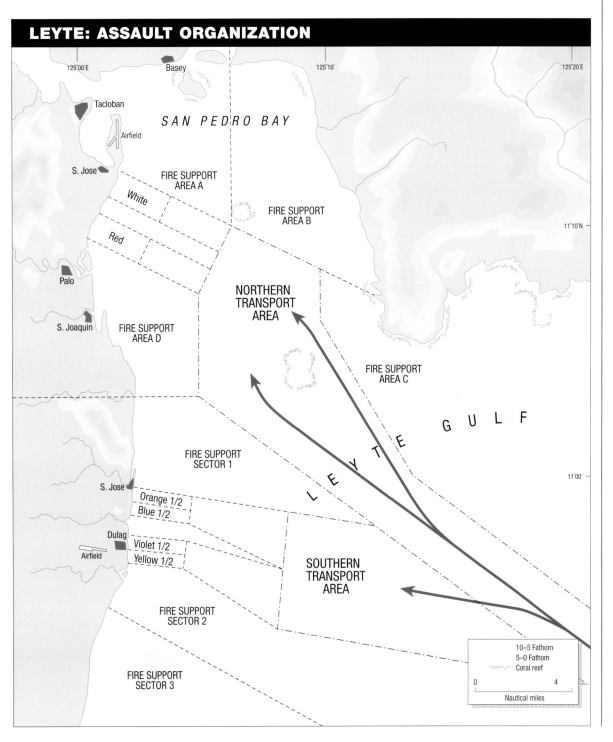

Very relevant to subsequent events was the actual wording of the
Operation Plan that Adm Nimitz issued to Adm Halsey. A critical
paragraph read 'The Joint Chiefs of Staff had directed that CINCPAC
[Adm Nimitz] furnish necessary fleet support to operations (including
Leyte and Western Samar) by forces of the South-West Pacific … Forces
of Pacific Ocean Areas will cover and support forces of South-West Pacific
… Western Pacific Task Forces [the Third Fleet] will destroy enemy naval
and air forces in or threatening the Philippines Area, and protect the air
and sea communications along the Central Pacific Axis … In case
opportunity for destruction of major portions of the enemy fleet offers or
can be created, *such destruction becomes the primary task* [author's italics] …'
When Halsey redrafted Nimitz' Operation Plan as an integral part of his
own operation orders to the Third Fleet, the italicized phrase survived
almost verbatim.

In view of the devastating effectiveness of American air power before
and during the operation, it is something of a surprise to discover how
complex and fragmented was its organization. Gen MacArthur controlled
not only the strike capacity of the Seventh Fleet's considerable force of
escort carriers (R Adm Thomas L. Sprague's TG 77.4) but also LtGen
George C. Kenney's (Army) Air Forces Southwest Pacific, currently
operating mainly from western New Guinea and its offshore island of
Morotai and Biak.

In addition to the enormous strike capacity of the Third Fleet carrier
groups (V Adm Marc. A. Mitscher's TF38) Adm Nimitz had responsibility
also for MajGen Willis H. Hale's VII Army Air Force, currently forward-
based in the Marianas. Where Kenney reported directly to MacArthur,
however, Hale's route to Nimitz was via V Adm John H. Hoover, who
headed Forward Areas Central Pacific Command.

To complicate matters, there were two further army air commands in
the theatre. Of these, the China-based XIV Army Air Force (MajGen
Claire L. Chennault) was part of Gen Joseph W. Stilwell's
China–Burma–India command. The other, the XX Army Air Force of

MajGen Curtis E. LeMay, answered through Gen H.H. Arnold to the JCS. This latter force comprised the new B-29 heavy bombers which operated first from India, then China before moving to the Marianas. Their ultimate function was the direct bombardment of Japan.

Deception has always been an important aspect of war and American policy was, to use their own famous phrase, 'to hit 'em where they ain't'. Thus, to confuse the Japanese as to the next objective, an American task group of three heavy cruisers and six destroyers carried out a sustained bombardment of tiny Marcus Island on 9 October. The island was too small and too isolated to have major strategic significance, however, and the enemy viewed the operation as no more than a nuisance raid.

With the near elimination of the German naval threat the British also were slowly assembling a new Pacific Fleet. Although enthusiastically supported by President Roosevelt and Prime Minister Churchill, this development was not popular in high circles of the US Navy for Adm Ernest J. King, the Chief of Naval Operation (CNO), was pursuing his own agenda. In order to justify the still enormous expansion of the US Navy (already largely unnecessary) he needed existing resources to appear stretched, and did not welcome British reinforcement. Adm Halsey understandably wanted the destruction of the Imperial Japanese Navy to be an all-American success, and simply wanted the British to be unable to claim that they had assisted.

Presidential wishes, however, could not be completely ignored and Adm King had the British stage a major diversion in the Indian Ocean. Air and surface bombardment in the Nicobars, 17–21 October, were intended to suggest that the forthcoming major blow would fall on the Malay Peninsula. The Japanese, however, were in no way deluded and made no resulting counter-deployments.

JAPANESE SHO-1 PLAN

Once the Battle of the Philippine Sea had denuded its carriers of trained aircrew, the Imperial Japanese Navy knew that it would have to await trained replacements before being able to engage the US Navy in the 'decisive battle' that doctrine demanded. The pace of the Allied advance, in both the central and south-west Pacific, was such, however, that the Japanese knew that a desperately required breathing space would not be granted them. All pointers indicated that the Philippines would be the next objective and that, of the four variations on the SHO-GO contingency plan, SHO-1 would be the one most likely to be implemented. It would have to be pursued with what forces were to hand, and it was recognized that, even if the Japanese fleet could entice the Third Fleet to action within range of land-based air power, it was unrealistic to expect decisive victory, for TF38 was simply too powerful.

V Adm Fukudome had not admitted to either Toyoda or Ozawa the true state to which land-based air had been reduced, but it was already accepted that any Allied invasion fleet would need to be destroyed by surface action rather than by air attack.

The Japanese plan thus centred on getting a sufficiently powerful force to the invasion zone. As the Third Fleet would prevent this, the obvious ploy was to lure it elsewhere. An irresistible bait existed in

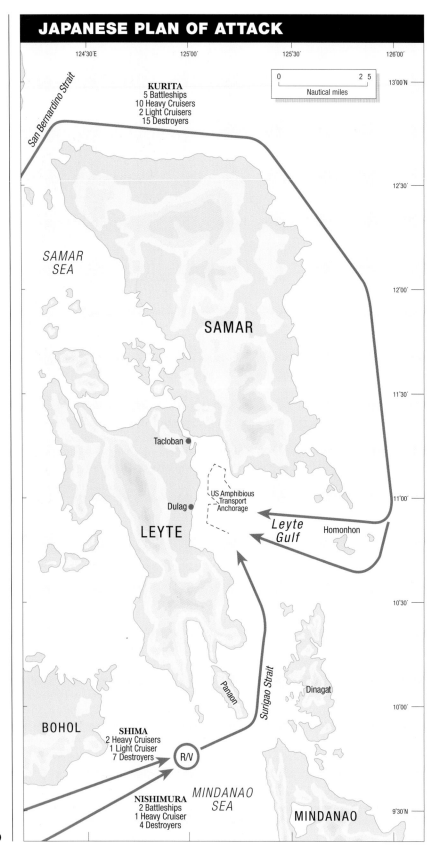

JAPANESE PLAN OF ATTACK

KURITA
5 Battleships
10 Heavy Cruisers
2 Light Cruisers
15 Destroyers

San Bernardino Strait

0   2 5
Nautical miles

13°00'N

12°30'

12°00'

11°30'

11°00'

10°30'

10°00'

9°30'N

124°30'E   125°00'   125°30'   126°00'

SAMAR SEA

SAMAR

Tacloban

US Amphibious Transport Anchorage

Dulag

LEYTE

Leyte Gulf

Homonhon

Panaon

Surigao Strait

Dinagat

BOHOL

SHIMA
2 Heavy Cruisers
1 Light Cruiser
7 Destroyers

R/V

MINDANAO SEA

NISHIMURA
2 Battleships
1 Heavy Cruiser
4 Destroyers

MINDANAO

Mitsubishi Zeros readying for take-off from a Japanese carrier. At Leyte, Japanese air power was not a significant factor in the battle, though the lure of aircraft carriers was used to good effect. (NARA)

Ozawa's toothless carrier force. It was no time to be considering long-term implications: the threat was imminent and, should the Philippines be lost, there would be little reason to have conserved the fleet.

Hastily modified to suit prevailing circumstances, SHO-1 now took the following form. Ozawa himself would lead the decoy carrier force, which would trail its coat to the north-east of Luzon, safely distant from the likely locations of Allied landings. Even if aware of the carriers' reduced striking power, Halsey would understand their potential and could be relied upon to go in their pursuit. With the Third Fleet's carrier groups thus safely removed, Japanese surface action groups would hit the invasion area at first light, arriving from north and south simultaneously.

Everything would require precise timing yet, at mid-October, it was not yet certain that the Philippines would be the objective and, if they were, exactly where the blow would land (although Leyte was considered most likely). It was thus too risky to make initial fleet dispositions yet, at the same time, reference to Map 1 on page 6 will reveal the scale of the problem, with the fleet divided between the home islands and Lingga, near Singapore.

Once it was confirmed that the Allied move was to be against the Philippines, Ozawa's decoy Northern Force would depart the Inland Sea for its station off Luzon. Simultaneously, the main surface fleet, under Kurita, would sortie from Lingga to a suitable anchorage in the western Philippines. Here, it would divide. Kurita, with the more powerful contingent, would proceed to form the northern jaw of the pincer charged with closing on the invasion zone. The weaker part, under Nishimura, would aim to arrive at the same time to attack from the south. As it lacked the necessary firepower, it was to be joined by a further force. This, under

V Adm Shima, would have to come all the way from Japan and loop to the west of the archipelago before effecting a junction.

Last-minute adaptations to SHO-1 caused major shortcomings, with the various Japanese commanders having little or no knowledge of each other's movements. Fukudome, for instance, was not ordered to cover Kurita's Centre Group, having been instructed only to use his air power to destroy the Allied landing force. Nishimura and Shima, who needed to combine to maximise their strength as the Southern Force, had received no instructions to do so. Shima was the senior commander, yet would fail to use his initiative to take charge of the situation.

For the moment, the Japanese watched and waited for the next Allied move.

ACTION AND REACTION

INITIAL MOVES (17–22 OCTOBER)

American intelligence appreciations prior to the Leyte landings were sketchy and inaccurate. The Japanese navy was thought to have 'no apparent intent to interfere'. Even as late as 23 October (A plus 3) its observed movements were thought to be no more than reinforcement sorties along the lines of the well-remembered Tokyo Express. In an appreciation of possible Japanese reaction to the landings, issued by Gen MacArthur's headquarters, it was stated specifically that approach by their fleet via either the San Bernardino or the Surigao Strait would be 'impractical because of navigational hazards and the lack of manoeuvering space'.

In contrast, the Japanese assessment appears remarkably precise, with Adm Toyoda's Navy Department at the Imperial General Headquarters predicting that the blow would fall in the Philippines during the final ten days of October. The likely location would be Leyte. Without certainty, however, the executive order for SHO-1 could not be given. The Japanese could only *react* to events and, bearing in mind the distances involved, a counter-blow would be belated, falling on an enemy already well-entrenched.

By this stage in the war it was very unlikely that operations on this scale by either side could achieve complete surprise, making deception and the wrong-footing of an opponent that much more important.

The approach to Leyte Gulf from the open sea to the east is constricted somewhat by several small islands. These afforded the Japanese useful locations for gun batteries and observation posts while confining any shipping to specific channels which could be, and indeed were, mined.

At first light on 17 October, therefore, companies of the 6th Ranger Battalion were landed on the islands and on the northern extremity of Dinagat to deal with any such enemy positions. Minesweepers moved in at the same time to clear the designated fairways. The weather was appalling, with winds gusting to a reported 60 knots, and incessant rain squalls reducing visibility to a half-mile. All the landing craft used by the Rangers broached in the heavy surf and became stranded.

These activities were sufficient to convince the Japanese of American intentions. The imminence of the blow had been confirmed by reconnaissance reports of shipping concentrations at Hollandia and Wakde in New Guinea (although the others at Manus and Ulithi had apparently gone unnoticed), and now had come the vital indication of time and place.

At 0809 on 17 October, therefore, Adm Toyoda issued an alert for SHO-1 to ships and units of the Japanese fleet. Still cautious about committing his forces irrevocably, however, he delayed transmission of the

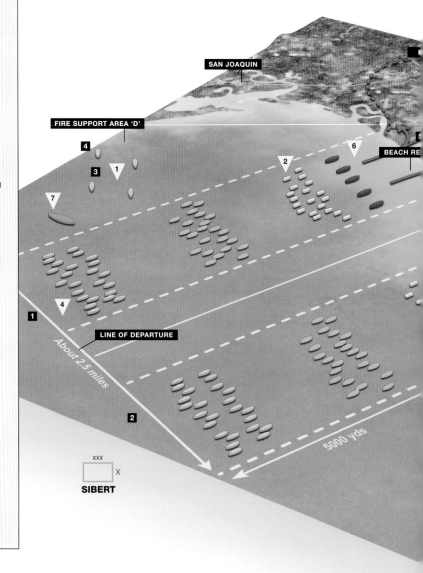

UNITS

1 TG78.1 Palo Attack Group (Barbey)
Transport Unit: Transdiv 24
4 Attack Transports (APA)
1 Attack Cargo Ship (AKA)
1 Transport
1 Landing Ship Dock (LSD)

Transdiv 6
3 Attack Transports (APA)
1 Attack Cargo Ship (AKA)
1 cargo ship
2 Landing Ship Dock (LSD)

Destroyer Screen: Desron 25
4 destroyers (DD)

Attached: LST Group 20 (Flotilla 7)
12 Landing Ship Tank (LST)

24th Infantry Division & 21st Regimental
Combat Team

**2 TG78.2 San Ricardo Attack Group
(Fechteler)**
Transport Unit: Transdiv 32
2 Attack Transports (APA)
1 Transport
1 Attack Cargo Ship (AKA)
1 Landing Ship Dock (LSD)

Transdiv 20
3 Attack Transports (APA)
1 Transport
1 Attack Cargo Ship (AKA)
1 Landing Ship Dock (LSD)

4 destroyers (DD)

Attached: LST Group 20 (Flotilla 7)
14 Landing Ship Dock (LSD)

Fire Support Group North (Weyler)
3 battleships (BB)
6 destroyers (DD)

1st Cavalry Division (Reinforced)

3 Control Vessels
4 Close Covering Group
5 19th Infantry Brigade
6 34th Infantry Brigade
7 5th Cavalry Regiment
8 12th Cavalry Regiment
9 7th Cavalry Regiment
10 8 destroyers

EVENTS

1. As minesweepers clear approaches (complete by 0715), Weyler's Fire Support Unit North carries out pre-landing bombardment (0700–0900). Carrier aircraft also attack hinterland until 0915. From 0900 until 1000 (H-hour) Berkey's Close Covering Group continue bombardment.

Eight destroyers on bombardment duty in Fire Support Area 'A'.

2. 0943: First line of assault craft leave Line of Departure. They are preceded by eleven LCI(R). These begin firing 1,200 yards from beaches, saturating the defences with 5,500 4.5-inch rockets. Landing on time at 1000, the wave headed by LVTs and flanked by LCI(G). Bombardment completed immediately ahead of touchdown, which is opposed only by small arms, MG and mortar fire.

3. 1000: At H-hour aircraft return to hit Guinhandang (Hill 522) which commands the flat hinterland.

4. Sixteen waves of LCA and LCVP land at approximately five-minute intervals, with craft returning to transports for re-loading. LSDs close toward LST anchorage to launch LVTs. LSTs ordered onto beach at 1045 while troops are still landing. The 8th Cavalry Regiment, in reserve, is landed on Beach White by 1130 and remains a reserve unit near San Jose.

5. First four waves land within 16 minutes.

6. Beach Red approaches prove to be too shallow to allow LSTs to beach close-in (no causeway units available). Four ground and are badly hit by mortar fire, as are several assault craft. LSTs, carrying 24 Div's artillery

and armour, are diverted to Beach White as space permits and to shore on Cataisan Peninsula, taken by 1600.

7. After midday on A-day, Gen MacArthur, Philippine President Osmena and entourage land from cruiser *Nashville* in his famous 'I have returned' routine.

8. Despite heavy fighting over boggy terrain inland of Beach Red, X Corps largely achieves its objective line by nightfall.

By 1730 on A-day, 18,500 troops and 13,500 tons of supplies have been landed.

NORTHERN LANDINGS, LEYTE 20 OCTOBER 1944 – 1000

The map shows the Leyte Gulf Northern Landing just before touchdown at 1000 on 20 October 1944. Out of frame to the left, beyond the line of departure, was the anchorage for all associated amphibious warfare shipping.

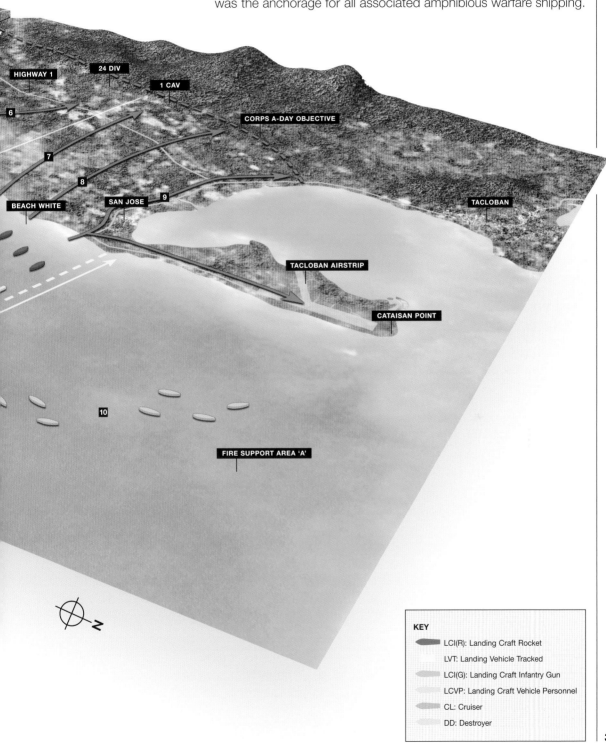

XX
16
MAKINO

HIGHWAY 1

24 DIV

1 CAV

6

CORPS A-DAY OBJECTIVE

7

8

BEACH WHITE

SAN JOSE

9

TACLOBAN

TACLOBAN AIRSTRIP

CATAISAN POINT

10

FIRE SUPPORT AREA 'A'

N

KEY

LCI(R): Landing Craft Rocket

LVT: Landing Vehicle Tracked

LCI(G): Landing Craft Infantry Gun

LCVP: Landing Craft Vehicle Personnel

CL: Cruiser

DD: Destroyer

executive order until 1110 on 18 October. This meant that the earliest time for the actual Japanese attack on the Allied amphibious fleet had to be set for first light on 22 October. Even this date then had to be set back a further three days, apparently by problems attendant upon loading the reduced airwings aboard Ozawa's carriers and the supply of fuel to those heavy units located in the Ryukyus.

Some 48 hours before the first of the Allied assault forces positioned themselves in the pre-dawn darkness of the Leyte Gulf, V Adm Kurita sailed from Lingga Roads. At 0100 on 18 October his flagship weighed and led to sea a truly formidable surface fighting force. Its mainspring was the pair of 68,000-ton super-battleships, *Yamato* and *Musashi*, whose size and main battery of nine 46cm (18.1in) guns would never be surpassed. In support were five older, but fully modernized, capital ships *Nagato*, *Fuso, Yamashiro, Kongo* and *Haruna,* 11 heavy and two light cruisers and 19 destroyers.

Kurita was bound for Brunei Bay, where his force arrived without incident. Here, it refuelled and awaited final orders, which arrived on the afternoon of 20 October, by which time the initial Allied assault on Leyte Gulf had been successfully concluded.

A few hours later, and far to the north, Ozawa's decoy Northern Force slipped unnoticed out of the Inland Sea. It was led by the fleet carrier *Zuikaku* which, as the only survivor of the six carriers that had ravaged Pearl Harbor, bore what the Americans term the 'Indian sign' – she was a marked ship. In company were three light carriers, two hybrid battleship/carriers (with no aircraft), three light cruisers and nine destroyers. In view of his force's role, it was ironic that Ozawa passed through the American submarine standing patrol line without being observed or reported.

Also starting from Japanese home waters was Shima's force. Already the weakest of the formations, it had been reduced by having several of

USS *Pennsylvania* demonstrates her prodigious fire power from 14in and 5in guns. Launched in 1913, the venerable battleship survived the Japanese attack at Pearl Harbor and was to become part of Adm Oldendorf's Bombardment and Fire Support Group positioned in the Surigao Strait. (NARA)

Troops approaching the landing beaches at Leyte watch the aerial battle above them. (NARA)

its units earmarked for a diversionary troop landing. Having received his stand-by signal on 21 October, Shima sailed the following day. His effective remaining force comprised two heavy and one light cruiser, and seven destroyers.

Shima's orders were ill-defined, charging him to 'support and cooperate' with Nishimura's group, which was hived off Kurita's main force at Brunei Bay. Kurita, with what we will term the Centre Group, sailed at 0800 on 22 October. This force had to synchronize its attack, at dawn on the 25th, with that of the Southern Force, yet it had further to travel. Nishimura thus remained at Brunei Bay with the battleships *Yamashiro* and *Fuso*, the heavy cruiser *Mogami* and four destroyers.

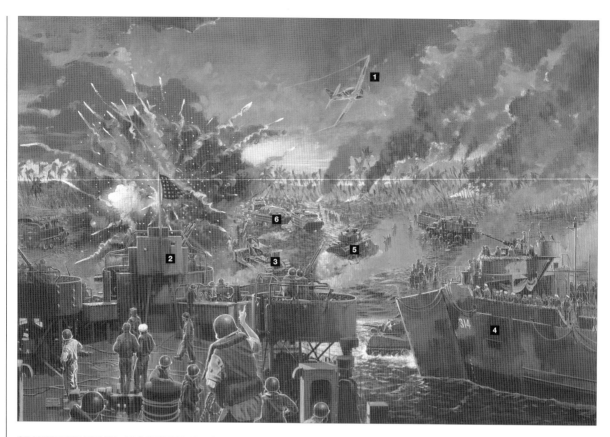

ORANGE TWO BEACH, 20 OCTOBER 1944 (pages 38–39)

Such was the scale of the amphibious assault on Leyte Gulf that it was divided into Northern and Southern Landings, the two separated by about 11 miles. The latter operation was the responsibility of V Adm Theodore S. Wilkinson's TF79, which put ashore XXIV Corps (7th and 96th Divisions) on a 5,000-yard front. On its far right were Orange One and Orange Two beaches, the latter having to its right the small rise of Liberanan Head, with the greater height of Catmon Hill looming beyond. It is the evening of 'A-day'. The initial assault went in ten hours earlier, successfully and almost unopposed. Sporadic enemy mortar fire from the high ground has caused some damage and casualties but has been quelled by the advance of forward units to their first-day objectives about three miles inland. The big transports laying offshore have been largely discharged and, the surviving assault craft recovered, the beach is now occupied by large landing craft. Early tensions have subsided and there is something of a relaxed atmosphere as the heavy equipment goes ashore in support of the 383rd Infantry Regiment of the 96th Division. Battered by days of relentless US carrier-based air strikes, Japanese airfields are, by now, almost denuded of aircraft but, although mauled, enemy air power cannot be assumed impotent. Suddenly, over the organized chaos of Orange Two, there is the roar of a low-flying aircraft. From the direction of the town of Dulag, to the left, a Zeke fighter bomber (1) banks steeply, its approach screened by smoke from fires still burning from the morning's pre-landing bombardment. Its two 60kg bombs hit the crowded beach area and the

incident is over in seconds, too quickly for the numerous, closed-up gun crews to react. With scarcely a valedictory shot being fired, at least one Japanese aviator lives to fight another day. Our observation point looks across the foredeck of a Landing Ship, Tank (LST) (2). In length 328 feet (100 metres), and displacing 4,080 tons fully loaded, an LST has a range of 6,000 miles and is well capable of making ocean voyages. Up to seven 40mm and twelve 20mm guns give them considerable defensive capability. Where a beach has a very shallow declivity, the LST bow doors may connect with floating causeways. Where these are not available, sand causeways may be thrown up by an armoured dozer (3). To our right is the distinctive forward end of a Landing Ship, Medium (LSM) (4), a smaller, 203.5 foot vessel with a load capacity of five medium or three heavy tanks. Through the deepening gloom of early dusk, the residual fires show brighter, their pall almost obscuring the Catmon heights. Following much Pacific experience, few personnel and little equipment is left to linger on the beach. Specialist gangs shift the unending cargoes of supplies and ammunition quickly and expertly, most heavy trucks having already ground their way inland. A few late Shermans (5) are coming ashore, their leader struggling as it bogs down in the soft sand. Adjacent to the beach exit are two of the invaluable DUKU, 2½-ton 6x6 amphibian trucks (6). Popularly known as 'Ducks', these vehicles can shift either 25 equipped troops or over two tons of cargo direct from ship to shore and, if required, beyond. Even as this continuous activity progresses, the whole operational Japanese fleet is concentrating, far to the west. The mortal challenge that it represents is still, however, four days distant.

US personnel and supplies continue to pour into Leyte. It was the largest amphibious operation to date in the Philippines. (Associated Press © EMPICS)

Ten Japanese submarines, already at sea around Formosa, were also ordered to the Leyte area, but most arrived too late to affect the main actions.

As the Japanese moved purposefully on their assigned missions, the Allied fleets, predominantly American, went about their pre-landing business. Hoping for a challenge from the whole Imperial Japanese Navy, Adm Halsey kept the Third Fleet to the east of Luzon, at no great distance from the location toward which Ozawa was, in fact, making.

The resulting absence of the fleet carriers left Thomas Sprague's escort carriers with the task of neutralizing enemy air bases in Mindanao and the Visayas for a space of three days, with the attendant attrition of aircraft, aircrew and stores. Following the actual landing, they would need to extend further in order to provide direct support for forces ashore.

Because of the nature of their designated shore targets, R Adm Oldendorf's battleships and cruisers had taken aboard a high proportion of common shell, in other words high explosive rather than armour-piercing or semi armour-piercing. In the pre-landing softening-up bombardments they had also expended a goodly proportion of their outfits.

KURITA'S CENTRE GROUP

Ambush in the Palawan Passage (21–23 October)

Before they sortied from Brunei Bay V Adm Kurita's commanding officers had been summoned aboard the flagship, the heavy cruiser *Atago*, for briefing. Their mission should have been straightforward. The enemy had landed in force; he needed to be defeated; they should sink his transports, therefore, isolating his still-limited military forces ashore

41

where they could be destroyed in detail. To the majority of Japanese officers, however, it was considered 'dishonourable' to molest 'soft' targets such as merchant shipping. Doctrine was that warships were meant to engage other warships in battle. Despite the dictates of common sense, therefore, Kurita sought and received agreement from Tokyo that, should the opportunity present itself, his force, covered by land-based air, would take on the Third Fleet's carrier force, TF38. Such a course would not only have negated the whole operation but would have been suicidal. As it happens, the opportunity did not arise, but the episode demonstrated dangerously muddled thinking.

Although well aware that the Japanese navy was on the move, the American high command had, at this stage, little idea of what or whither. Movements so far were beyond the range of search aircraft from Mitscher's carriers and within only the occasional coverage of US Navy PB4Y Liberators working out of Morotai, nearly 800 miles distant. Over a dozen American submarines were, however, in Philippine waters and it was this service (SubSoWesPac, part of Gen MacArthur's more peripheral responsibilities) that made first contact and drew first blood.

Over 200 miles long, yet averaging less than 20 wide, the attenuated island of Palawan is aligned approximately north-east/south-west and, together with islets that fall in line at either end, gives the impression of once having been a land bridge between Borneo and the Philippine archipelago. Any navigator bound from Brunei Bay (in north-west Borneo) to the central Philippines, and constrained by time factors from adopting any evasive routing, would naturally take the track along the western coast of Palawan. As did Kurita.

This route, known as the Palawan Passage, is relatively straight-forward for navigation but is limited in width for, running parallel with the island, there is a shallow, reef-strewn area labelled on the chart simply as 'Dangerous Grounds'. Somewhat confined, and replete with uncharted hazards, the Palawan Passage was not the most relaxing billet for an extended submarine patrol but, on the other hand, any enemy vessel in transit was certain to be noticed. In this tactically important area were stationed two American submarines, *Darter* and *Dace*.

At midnight, 22–23 October the two boats were surfaced, cloaked in the calm, velvety blackness, as their two skippers conferred by megaphone. Their conversation was interrupted at 0016 when *Darter*'s radar watch reported a contact. Within a few minutes, the plot revealed it to be a substantial body of ships, approaching on a course slightly north of north-east. There were no known friendly forces due in the area, so the consensus was to wait until daylight to evaluate the composition of the group.

At 0245, although still dark, the *Darter*'s men could make out the formation as they paralleled it at 15 knots. Just 20,000 yards distant was a submariner's dream, a huge assembly of warships, the targets overlapping. Kurita was steaming in two main columns, each in two parts and comprising battleships led by two or three heavy cruisers. Probably due to the constriction of the passage, his destroyers were also disposed in columns rather than in the form of a conventional antisubmarine screen.

The two American boats moved ahead of the enemy into an attacking position and, with a light cruiser and two destroyers heading

directly for him, the skipper of the *Darter*, Cdr McClintock, lined up on the leading cruiser of the port column in the dim light of first dawn. It was Kurita's poor luck that McClintock had selected his flagship, *Atago*.

Too close to miss, the *Darter* scored with at least four of her six bow torpedoes. Without waiting to observe the result, McClintock furiously swung his boat about to present his four stern tubes. These were loosed at the second cruiser in line. She, the *Takao*, shuddered under the impact of two of them.

As *Darter* went as deep as the channel permitted and began to endure an hour of, by all accounts, not-too-accurate depth charging, her sound gear picked up a further series of detonations. This was the noise of the *Dace* attacking the starboard column. Here, four more hits had immediately destroyed the third in line, the heavy cruiser *Maya*.

The *Atago*, meanwhile, was mortally damaged, going down in about 18 minutes and obliging Kurita and his staff to swim for it. Sorely injured, the *Takao* fell out of line and reversed course to head painfully for Brunei. Although left with an escort, the big cruiser made an irresistible target. However, intent on stalking her, the skipper of the *Darter* put his boat firmly aground. She was soon exposed, stranded on a shoal and, unable to refloat her, the *Dace* took on her crew and did her best to destroy her before leaving. Hopelessly overcrowded with two crews aboard, the *Dace* made it to Australia.

Not only had the two boats severely mauled the Japanese Centre Group they had also gravely dented its flag officer's confidence as, one of a limited number of survivors, he was pulled from the sea by a destroyer and transferred to the battleship *Yamato*. His vital communications personnel had either been killed, scattered around the fleet or were returning in the shattered *Takao*.

Bent on pursuing his schedule, Kurita pressed on, but his force and composition were now known. By midnight, 23–24 October the formation was heading eastward toward Mindoro and, as daylight strengthened on the 24th, it rounded the island's southern tip to enter the Sibuyan Sea.

Kurita had been bloodied but was still dangerous, on time, and headed for the critical San Bernardino Strait. It was now Adm Halsey's job to stop him.

KURITA'S CENTRE GROUP

Battle of the Sibuyan Sea (24 October)

Halsey's characteristic outlook led him to consider his Third Fleet in purely 'offensive' terms. He viewed Kinkaid's reinforced Seventh Fleet as 'defensive' and of a strength sufficient to take care of any direct threat.

Having spent days off a hostile coast chastising Japanese airfields with no response from the enemy battle fleet, Halsey considered his opponent's land-based air a spent force, and report of Kurita's progress from Singapore produced in him the firm opinion that the group would operate to the *west* of the Philippines, in general support of Japanese military forces.

Overly anxious to tangle with Kurita's force, Halsey was sharply reminded by Nimitz that his job was to remain in support of MacArthur's Southwest Pacific forces, and he was explicitly forbidden to enter the archipelago.

V Adm Mitscher, tactical Commander of the Third Fleet's carrier groups, had, together with his charges, been almost continuously at sea for about nine months, and sheer fatigue in both had begun to reduce morale and efficiency. Not customarily one to complain, Mitscher now made strong representations to Halsey. Always responsive to the needs of his men, the latter took the view that, as he was now prohibited from seeking out his enemy (i.e. to the *west* of the islands), he would release his carrier groups, in rotation, to return to the fleet facility at Ulithi Atoll for rest, replenishment and refurbishment.

Accordingly, at 2030 on 22 October (less than four hours before the *Darter*'s first contact with Kurita's group) V Adm MacCain's TG38.1 was ordered away to Ulithi, with R Adm Davison's TG38.4 to follow the next day. Their scheduled return on 29 October would release the other pair of task groups for their turn.

The *Darter*'s incoming reports did not cause Halsey to re-assess Japanese intentions, but he did take the precaution of cancelling TG38.4s planned departure. All three carrier groups were ordered to refuel and to close the Philippines.

By dawn on 24 October R Adm Sherman's TG 38.3, was off Luzon, R Adm Bogan's TG 38.2 (incorporating Halsey's flagship, *New Jersey*) was east of the San Bernardino Strait, while Davison's TG38.4 was abreast of Leyte Gulf. All launched reconnaissance at the earliest possible moment to establish the new position, course and speed of the *Darter*'s reported fleet.

Heading toward the area east of the Philippines, where Halsey calculated that the Japanese would be, an aircraft from the TG 38.2 carrier *Intrepid* located Kurita at 0625 by chance and where he actually was, rounding the southern tip of Mindoro. A surprised Halsey had to accept that Kurita was, in fact, headed for the San Bernardino and was going to

The formidable Centre Force, commanded by Adm Kurita, leaves Brunei Bay, Borneo, on 22 October 1944, heading for the Philippines. Right to left: battleships *Nagato*, *Musashi* and *Yamato*; heavy cruisers *Maya*, *Chokai*, *Takao*, *Atago*, *Haguro* and *Myoko*. It was to have a surprise encounter with US escort carriers. (NARA)

offer battle. He immediately ordered both Sherman and Davison to close Bogan's group at their best speed.

While this order was being complied with, one of Davison's scout aircraft, combing the southern sector, reported a new Japanese fleet, heading east across the Sulu Sea. This was Nishimura's van group of the Southern Force and Halsey again made a correct assessment, i.e. that it, too, was bound for Leyte Gulf, but this time via the Surigao Strait to its south. Although his latest orders to the carrier groups were taking Davison's, the southernmost carrier group, beyond the range at which he could engage it, Halsey remained confident that Kinkaid had means sufficient to deal with the problem posed by Nishimura. TG38.4 continued to move northward.

An important point that needs to be understood is that the autocratic Gen MacArthur, insistent upon maintaining the independence of his command, forbade any direct means of communication between the Third and Seventh Fleets. In short, Halsey and Kinkaid could not confer directly. Signals between them were required to be encoded and transmitted to the main fleet radio station at Manus. From here they were re-transmitted on what was known as the Fox schedule. Every ship had to copy each complete set of transmissions but decode only those signals preceded with its own call-sign. The days of battle around the Philippines generated huge levels of radio traffic, so much of it prefixed 'Urgent' that this indicator became virtually meaningless. Messages between the admirals could thus take hours, arrive out of sequence or even fail to arrive at all. With the lack of a common superior in the theatre, the two commanders were unable to operate in close coordination.

Dawning clear and bright, the morning of 24 October saw Mitscher's three task groups ranged down the eastern side of the Philippines – Sherman to the north, Bogan (with Halsey) in the centre and Davison to the south. With a battle looming, the admiral took the precaution of recalling McCain's group, now 300 miles away en route to Ulithi. McCain's was the most powerful of the four groups, but its return would necessarily be slowed by a refuelling rendezvous.

Throughout the night, Sherman's formation had been dogged by an enemy night-flying reconnaissance aircraft, about which he could do

The cruiser USS *Reno* at the stern of the carrier USS *Princeton* in a vain attempt to put out her fires. Shortly afterwards, *Princeton* exploded and sank, 24 October 1944. (NARA)

USS *Princeton* hit by a Japanese bomb, while the cruiser USS *Reno* passes in the foreground, 24 October 1944. (NARA)

nothing. It presaged a series of early air attacks, whose half-trained pilots were dealt with severely by the standing daylight combat air patrol (CAP). None the less, a single bomb-hit was made on the thin-skinned CVL *Princeton*. The ship was soon racked by fire and explosion, abandoned by all except fire-fighting parties.

The struggle to save the *Princeton* lasted until late afternoon and was, ultimately, unsuccessful. This diversion prevented Sherman from properly supporting the other groups. He assisted them considerably, however, in drawing the bulk of the land-based Japanese air attacks, together with the only weak air strike that could be mounted by Ozawa's Northern Force. This, of course, was still trying to draw attention to itself but, ironically, in the general mayhem, the

Americans failed to register that some of the attacking aircraft were carrier types. Ozawa remained unlocated.

Sherman felt secure in his private war because his group included the carrier *Lexington*, Mitscher's flagship, and it was Mitscher that had to absorb Halsey's justified criticism. Halsey, however, had an unfortunate habit of by-passing Mitscher to issue instructions directly to the task group commanders.

Early air searches mounted by Bogan and Davison located the forces of Kurita, Nishimura and Shima. None of them, to Halsey's consternation, contained carriers.

With Sherman drawing most of Fukudome's venom, Bogan and Davison concentrated on dealing with the largest of the enemy formations, that of Kurita. From 0810, when the Japanese were sighted in the Tablas Strait, they were hit by a series of air strikes. These, going in at 1026, 1245, 1330, 1415 and 1550, comprised a total of 259 sorties. They were mounted by various combinations of carriers and consisted of divebombers and torpedo bombers covered by fighters. Attacks went in through intense anti-aircraft fire, which claimed 18 aircraft.

The lack of a protective CAP over Kurita as he battled his way across the enclosed Sibuyan Sea was the result of Fukudome's conviction that his aircraft best served their purpose by attacking the American carriers directly. While this resulted in the loss of the *Princeton*, however, it left the other two groups untroubled and Kurita vulnerable.

Within the Centre Group, the huge *Yamato* and *Musashi* stood out. The latter accumulated significant damage and, falling out under escort, became something of an Aunt Sally. Her eventual sinking was a major success for carrier aircraft but she had attracted so much of the fire that, although several other ships took damaging bomb hits, only one other (the heavy cruiser *Myoko* with a torpedo hit) was obliged to drop out.

After the third air strike, Kurita briefly lost confidence, reversing course and losing a vital four hours or so before again, at 1715, assuming his easterly track for the strait. For various reasons his force had been

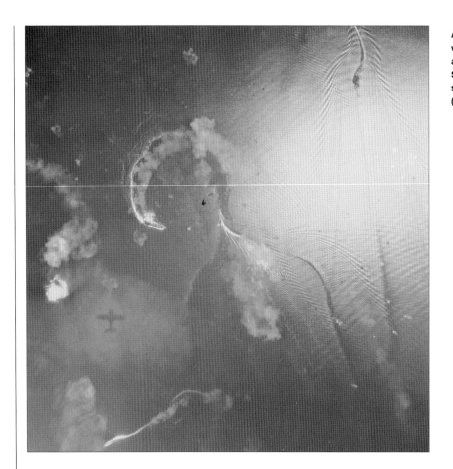

reduced by a battleship, four heavy cruisers and several destroyers left behind as escorts, and so on. He remained, however, in considerable force and a potent threat.

Halsey's returning aviators were in exuberant spirits. Having suffered comparatively few losses, they fell into the usual trap of over-optimistic assessment of their results. With several aircraft attacking at a time, it was not unusual for all to claim a hit, so that one success became several. Experienced intelligence officers should have allowed for this in debriefing, while Halsey, the most experienced of all, might have expected a degree of hyperbole. He preferred, however, to believe that Kurita's Centre Group no longer represented a threat. His mind was elsewhere for, somewhere out there, yet unaccounted for, were the Japanese carriers. These were what he wanted to destroy.

At 1512, following some deliberation, Halsey transmitted a 'Battle Plan', addressed to Mitscher, V Adm Willis A. Lee (the battleship commander) and the task group commanders. It was copied to Nimitz and Adm King (the CNO) but not to Kinkaid.

The signal warned Lee to be prepared to form a surface action group, to bear the tally TF34 and to be drawn from the non-aviation elements of TG 38.2 and 38.4 At 1710 he sent an amplifying signal: 'If the enemy sorties [i.e. through the San Bernardino Strait] TF34 will be formed when directed by me'. This message was received neither by Nimitz nor by King. Kinkaid, who had 'overheard' the 1512 transmission, also missed that of 1710.

Battleship *Yamato* is hit by a bomb near her forward turret while under attack in the Sibuyan Sea. She survived the attack. (NARA)

OZAWA'S NORTHERN FORCE

Ozawa located (24 October)

For V Adm Ozawa, his mission was painful. In normal times his carriers would have deployed upward of 250 aircraft and he, their admiral, would have been aggressively seeking confrontation with the enemy. Now virtually impotent, his squadron mustering barely 100 part-trained aircrew, his role was simply to be discovered by Third Fleet search aircraft then, using his precious carriers as live bait, to lure Halsey as far north as possible, clearing the way for Kurita to sweep Leyte Gulf clean of amphibious shipping. Intelligent and dedicated, Ozawa none the less accepted the importance of his mission and, if it involved total sacrifice, that was the price that would be paid.

Having left the Inland Sea on 20 October the Northern Force had kept well to the west to avoid being spotted by American reconnaissance aircraft already operating out of Saipan in the Marianas. Ozawa did not wish to be located until Kurita was well advanced, for his early destruction would achieve nothing.

It was, in fact, one of Ozawa's search aircraft that made first contact, sighting Sherman's group as early as 0820 on 24 October. The range still being too great, the Japanese commander headed southward until 1145 before launching 76 aircraft at the Americans from a little over 200 miles. This was the means by which Ozawa sought to announce his presence but, as has been recounted, Sherman's units were already deeply pre-occupied with repelling Fukudome's air attacks and in trying to save the crippled *Princeton*. Unremarked, Ozawa's aircraft followed instructions and flew on to Luzon rather than back to their carriers.

Ozawa had made his bid, knew not of what damage his aircraft had inflicted and remained unaware that his presence was still unsuspected. Lack of any American interest, however, raised his suspicions.

THE SINKING OF THE *MUSASHI*, 24 OCTOBER 1944
(pages 50–51)

By a very considerable margin, the Japanese battleships *Musashi* and *Yamato* were the greatest ever built. Their design displacement of 69,000 tons eclipsed the *Iowa*'s 52,000 tons. Their nine 46cm (18.1in) guns were the largest of modern times, comparing with the American's 16in. Their armoured citadel included a side belt of 410mm (16.1in) and a 200–380mm (7.9–15in) protective main deck. Much slower than their American peers, they would, none the less, have proved very difficult to defeat in a gunnery duel. As if to signal the end of the big-gun era, however, they were both sunk, not by shellfire but by overwhelming air attack, of which the primary weapon was the torpedo. On 24 October 1944 both of these behemoths formed the core of V Adm Kurita's Centre Group, bound for the American landing beaches of Leyte Gulf. Already bloodied, this force required en route to cross the Sibuyan Sea. This brought it to within diminishing range of two US Third Fleet carrier groups, R Adm Bogen's TG 38.2 and R Adm Davison's TG 38.4. During the day, 259 sorties were flown against Kurita's force, which enjoyed little or no air cover. The two big battleships attracted the brunt of the attacker's aggression and, once already injured and trailing, the *Musashi* fell out of formation. Struck by a claimed 19 torpedoes and 17 bombs, besides 16 damaging near-misses, the ship was ordered to be beached in order to save her. The picture depicts the *Musashi* at about 1915 on what was a calm October evening. The cruiser *Tone*, ordered to stand by, has found the great ship impossible to tow and has pulled out, leaving just two destroyers to assist. Aboard the ship, all power has failed and flooding between ruptured compartments is uncontrollable and remorselessly progressive. With no power, the ship's great guns remain paralysed at the position where they last fired, ironically in barrage fire to deter torpedo aircraft. Secondary mountings likewise point blindly and impotently at the now-peaceful sky. Only small hand-worked automatic guns remain operative. The effect of bombs, although mainly superficial, has been to ignite widespread fires below. With power having failed, these can no longer be fought and a gathering haze of smoke issues from numerous apertures. Settling by the head, and with a rapidly increasing list to port, the ship has become dangerously unstable and, well beyond the sanctuary of shallow waters, obviously has limited time left to her. Recognizing the inevitable, the flag captain, on behalf of the dead R Adm Inoguchi, has ordered the ship abandoned. The crew were mustered aft to salute the lowering of the ensign, and the emperor's portrait has been brought topside to be saved. As the destroyer *Kiyoshimo* (1) circles on anti-submarine watch, her speed low to avoid her sonar being masked by water noise, her consort, *Hamakaze* (2), has been ordered alongside for rescue purposes. Dismissed, the battleship's 2,500-strong crew move forward, urgently but without panic, to where the *Hamakaze* will lay her bow alongside. As the sun dips to the horizon, the golden chrysanthemum on the *Musashi*'s stern head dips into the sea. Within twenty minutes, it and she will be history.

Accordingly, at 1430, he detached his two hybrid battleship/carriers *Ise* and *Hyuga* (each lacking aircraft but still mounting eight 14in guns), together with a light escort, to make a direct challenge. To attack a fully active carrier task group in this way was truly sacrificial, yet the flag officer, R Adm Matsuda Chiaki, undertook the task without demur.

Matsuda was successful inasmuch as he was sighted at 1540 by a pair of aircraft from Davison's group which, together with Bogan's, was still occupied in flying strikes against Kurita as he advanced across the Sibuyan Sea. Land-based Japanese air activity was tailing off and Sherman was able to follow up the sighting by putting up further search aircraft. This, at 1640, finally located Ozawa, reporting the Northern Force's composition as four carriers, two light cruisers and about five destroyers. As all his force had now been sighted, Ozawa recalled Matsuda to re-concentrate the formation.

Halsey was now in something of a quandary. Ozawa's position was almost 200 miles north of his northernmost carrier group, i.e. Sherman's TG 38.3. It was too late to launch a strike and have the aircraft return in daylight (night flying was still a speciality). Left to himself, Ozawa might pull further to the north and use his already longer-range aircraft in a shuttle-bombing attack, flying from their carriers to airfields in Luzon, refuelling and re-arming before flying back to their ships, attacking Sherman on both legs of the flight.

As Halsey reviewed them, his options were:

(i)   To form TF34 as indicated and leave it, with one carrier group, to guard the San Bernardino Strait, while the other two carrier groups tackled Ozawa;
(ii) To hold back the whole strength of TF38 to guard the strait, or
(iii) To take the whole of TF38 north to make certain of destroying the Japanese carriers, the most potent force in their fleet.

Option (i) was dismissed as two carrier groups might not have been sufficient to destroy an enemy force of undetermined size. The second option was unthinkable in that it would leave the enemy carriers to fight another day, while placing the whole of TF38 between those carriers and hostile shore bases.

Gambling that Kurita was, as reported, a spent force, Halsey summoned R Adm 'Mick' Carney, his Chief of Staff, and gave the fateful order: 'Mick, start 'em north'.

HALSEY'S THIRD FLEET

Halsey's decision (24–25 October)

His mind made up, Adm Halsey ordered Bogan and Davison, at 2022 on 24 October, to concentrate on Sherman's group and to move north to attack Ozawa at dawn on the 25th. For good measure, he also instructed the returning McCain's TG 38.1 to refuel as quickly as possible and to rejoin the task force.

To crown a successful career, Halsey was determined to direct a major action from the bridge of his flagship. As a partisan scientist may 'prove' his hypothesis by ignoring all data that does not agree with it, so Halsey chose not to establish for certain that Kurita's Centre Group was, indeed, finished. Inexplicable was his decision to commit the whole of the Third Fleet to Ozawa's destruction. It was just what the Japanese had intended. How well they gauged their man.

Between them, his group had discovered and reported the full strength of the Northern Force, at that stage still split. Why should Halsey have doubted that this was the total enemy strength when, hours before, he had accepted the inflated aviators' reports of damage to Kurita? Had he chosen his second option, he would have set four attack and four light carriers, all with full air wings, on half that number of Japanese, whose remaining aircraft were now ashore. Mitscher would still have enjoyed overwhelming force, while the San Bernardino Strait would have been adequately guarded by a balanced surface/air action group.

Instead, by midnight on 24–25 October, the whole of the Third Fleet was heading northward at high speed. The CVL *Independence* of Bogan's group had a specialist night-flying unit. Its aircraft took one last look at Kurita's force and reported that, not only was it still headed eastward toward the strait but also, significantly, all navigation lights in this narrow waterway had been switched on.

Halsey's group commanders, including Lee of the battle group, already unhappy at their admiral's decision, were now truly worried. Most sagely kept their misgivings to themselves; those who chose to demur had their opinions brusquely acknowledged but not acted upon. As Halsey reported, late on the 25th: 'It seemed childish to me to guard statically San Bernardino Strait … [as] I believed that the Centre Force had been so heavily damaged … that it could no longer be considered a threat to the Seventh Fleet.'

While Halsey took a well-earned spell of sleep, Carney transmitted details of the situation: 'Strike reported indicate

A Japanese airman desperately clambers from the canopy of a dive bomber, seconds before his plane hits the sea.

USS *New Jersey* was the flagship of Adm Halsey. Launched in 1942, *New Jersey* was decoyed north, allowing the Japanese Centre Force to enter the San Bernardino Strait. (NARA)

Planes from USS *Intrepid* attacked Adm Kurita's Centre Force, damaging the battleship *Yamato* and sinking her sister ship, *Musashi*. *Intrepid*'s aircraft also attacked the Japanese carriers *Zuiho* and *Zuikaku*. *Intrepid* was later struck by a kamikaze attack, though she was soon repaired. (NARA)

enemy force Sibuyan Sea heavily damaged. Am proceeding north with three groups to attack enemy force at dawn.' All recipients interpreted this, taken in conjunction with earlier signals, as meaning only the three *carrier* groups, i.e. the aforementioned TF34 being left to cover the exit from the strait.

It will be recalled, however, that neither Nimitz nor King had received the 1710 signal amplifying Halsey's intentions. Although, as part of MacArthur's command, Kinkaid had not been an addressee, he had in fact received the first, i.e. 1512, message. Now given a transcript of Carney's transmission he, too, assumed that the heavy ships of TF34 remained interposed between his transports and the strait.

Halsey's signal phraseology was never noted for its precision but, on this occasion, it was very precise. The recipients overlooked that his flagship was the battleship *New Jersey*, a unit of the proposed TF34 and, as the signal clearly stated 'Am proceeding north …', it could really have meant only one thing.

The three carrier groups duly rendezvoused at 2345, at the very time that a surprised and relieved Kurita was threading his Centre Group through the now unwatched and unguarded San Bernardino Strait. Halsey was now focused on nailing Ozawa and, ignoring the risk that the enemy might detect them (and, by inference, him) by radar, he ordered away night-flying search aircraft. These confirmed, a little after 0200, not only Ozawa's presence but also that the Japanese were barely one hundred miles ahead.

Capt Arleigh Burke, late successful destroyer leader and now Mitscher's Chief of Staff, suggested that, to avoid the risk of the vulnerable carriers blundering into heavy enemy units before dawn, it would be wise to form TF34 promptly and to have it stationed ahead as a battle line. Halsey accepted the advice and, at 0240, Lee's ships pulled away at high speed.

Halsey informed Nimitz, King, MacArthur and Kinkaid of the move, the last two recipients indirectly. His signal terminated in a rather enigmatic 'Own force in three groups concentrated'. Kinkaid must have received the message quickly for at 0312, obviously uncertain of what Halsey really meant, he posed the direct question: 'Is TF34 guarding the San Bernardino Strait?'

Again, indirect signal routing proved to be the bogey for Halsey did not receive this pointed query until 0648. At 0704 he answered unequivocally: 'Negative. Task Force 34 is with carrier groups now engaging enemy carrier force.' Kinkaid was totally dismayed but, within minutes, it would get worse.

KURITA'S CENTRE GROUP

The Battle off Samar (25 October)

V Adm Kurita was now well behind schedule, thanks to his temporary reversal of course due to the heavy pressure of the Third Fleet's air strikes. There was no longer any hope of synchronizing his attack on Leyte Gulf with that of Nishimura and Shima from the south.

At 2145 on the 24th Kurita had radioed Toyoda: 'Will pass through San Bernardino at 0100 October 25th … reaching Leyte Gulf at about 1100.' The last was somewhat optimistic in that he expected to find an American force barring his exit from the strait.

At 2320 the last of the *Independence*'s night-fliers parted company with the Japanese force as they were re-directed by Halsey to locate Ozawa's Northern Force. Their reports of the Centre Group's progress had been transmitted, mainly for Kinkaid's benefit but, thanks to the cumbersome Third/Seventh Fleet communications system, there is no record that Kinkaid ever received them.

By 0035 on the 25th the whole of the Centre Group had exited the strait and, surprised at the lack of even an American picket there, Kurita cracked on down the coast of Samar, on the shortest route to his objective.

V Adm Kinkaid possessed within his Seventh Fleet very considerable firepower, a contributory factor in Halsey's decision making. Its

strength, however, was vested in ships intended to support amphibious warfare, not to fight major actions. Its battleships were all over-age veterans and its carriers all CVEs.

Converted from a variety of mercantile hulls, escort carriers (CVE) were intended for second-line tasks – convoy escort, anti-submarine patrol, training, ferrying and, as at Leyte Gulf, mounting air support for forces ashore. Compared with a 900-foot 33-knot fleet carrier, a CVE was under 500 feet in length and capable of only 18 knots. Importantly, she deployed only about two dozen aircraft against one hundred.

CVEs had operational limitations, particularly in their modest speed which, in calm conditions, could make it difficult to generate sufficient wind-over-deck to get a heavily-laden aircraft airborne. Their hulls were also too small to include what would normally be considered adequate protection and safety arrangements for the large quantities of aviation fuel and ordnance carried under operational conditions.

The Seventh Fleet CVEs were organized as Task Group 77.4 (i.e. TG 77.4). This was subdivided into three task units, namely TU77.4.1 (R Adm Thomas L. Sprague, TG77.4's senior officer), TU77.4.2 (R Adm Felix B. Stump) and TU77.4.3 (R Adm Clifton A.F. 'Ziggy' Sprague, no relation). For voice radio purposes, each unit had a call sign. These, in order, were Taffy 1, 2 and 3, and it was by these that the task units were usually known.

The normal establishment of each task unit was six CVEs, with a screen of three destroyers (DD) and four destroyer escorts (DE), but, on 25 October Taffy 1 was reduced to four carriers, two having been detached to Morotai the day before.

Equipped only for daylight flying, the three task units were kept extremely busy pending the establishment of airfields ashore. They were required to maintain a combat air patrol (CAP) over the beachhead, and an anti-submarine (AS) patrol to seaward. They provided on-call air support for the army and kept up a steady stream of attacks on enemy airstrips, dumps and targets of opportunity, such as road convoys.

At full strength, each task unit could deploy about 150 aircraft. The units worked independently with, perhaps, 50 miles between them. On the morning of 25 October, Taffy 1 was the southernmost, operating off northern Mindanao. Taffy 2 was directly east of Leyte Gulf, while Taffy 3 was to its north, off the coast of Samar and directly in the path of Kurita's Centre Group.

V Adm Kinkaid had been up all night, as reports came in regularly regarding the progress of the Japanese Southern Force (see below). At 0155 and as yet only with reservations about whether Halsey was holding the ring to the north, he ordered Thomas Sprague to conduct air searches from dawn. They were to include the sector from 340 to 030 degrees (i.e. from about NNW to NNE).

Taffy 2 was best prepared, with Sprague issuing the necessary instructions to Stump at 0330. Receipt of this order was timed at 0430, which meant that the instructions to the CVE concerned was not despatched until 0509. Sunrise was at 0630 but daylight was well advanced by the time that the necessary ten aircraft were airborne. The last took the air at 0658.

'Ziggy' Sprague's Taffy 3, off Samar, had stood-to more promptly that morning but, in accordance with routine, had sent its aircraft southward and eastward. By 0530 it had put a 12-plane CAP over the beachhead and, by 0610, had flown off a six-plane AS patrol. The day's routine established, Taffy 3's duty crews could be stood-down for breakfast.

As daylight strengthened on the morning of 25 October, V Adm Kurita became increasingly apprehensive. During the previous 48 hours he had survived having his flagship sunk under him, but had lost track of many of his trusted staff. He had been strafed, bombed and torpedoed for hours by almost unopposed airstrikes, and had been obliged to leave the stricken *Musashi* to her fate. The strength of the enemy and the lack of friendly air cover had obliged him to reverse course. His protests to Toyoda had met only with the general exhortation that 'All forces [will] dash to the attack'.

Now, suspiciously, as if encouraging him on, he had been allowed to pass an unguarded choke point and gazed at an empty horizon. Beyond lay his objective, its presence all too evident from incessant radio chatter. Above flew not so much as a single reconnaissance aircraft.

Not surprisingly, Kurita was certain that the Third Fleet was lurking close at hand and, shortly, the whole of its mighty air strength would be hurled at him. His doubts seemed to be realized when, within minutes, his radars detected aerial activity ahead. At 0627 as the sun rose on a clear morning, Kurita changed his force's disposition from night cruising order to an anti-aircraft formation. Even as the smaller units were positioning themselves around the larger, lookouts reported the horizon ahead to be peppered with masts. Within minutes came the unwelcome news that the masts were those of aircraft carriers.

His fears realized, Kurita resolved to sell his force's existence for as high a price as possible. Already, he reasoned, the carrier groups ahead would be getting their strikes airborne. With no time to waste, he countermanded his earlier order for his force's redisposition and, instead, signalled 'General Attack', an instruction for each commanding officer to work independently. In place of a formidable battle line of

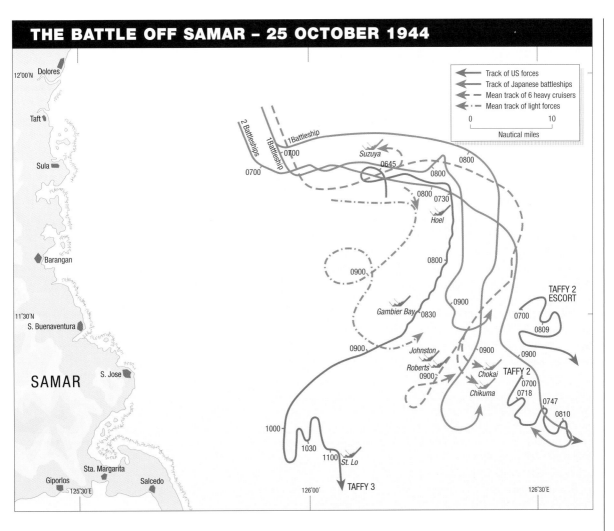

four battleships and six heavy cruisers, Kurita's ships were rushing pell-mell at what was assumed to be an overwhelming enemy force.

In fact, Kurita had seen only what he had expected to see. What lay in his path was not the Third Fleet, which Halsey had taken far to the north, but the escort carriers of 'Ziggy' Sprague's Taffy 3.

It was a bright morning with about 30 per cent cumulus cloud and the occasional mild rain squall. At 0645 an American aircraft reported that it was being fired upon by a strange force of warships. These were already appearing on Sprague's radar and now the flak was clearly visible. Observers expressed disbelief as the massive Japanese super-structures eased above the horizon. At 0658 the vivid stabs of their opening salvoes galvanized the Americans to action.

As the first lines of shell splashes marched across his force, Sprague ordered a course change to the east, which opened the range while allowing him to launch aircraft. All ships were ordered to make smoke, the calm humid atmosphere soon supporting the black, oily barriers, interlaced with grey-black chemical smoke. Urgent pleas for assistance were broadcast *en clair*.

Friendly forces reacted quickly, but Taffy 1 was about 130 miles distant, Taffy 2 fifty. All carriers despatched aircraft in a 'come-as-youare' mode. From his headquarters ship, Kinkaid had his fighter detection unit send all airborne aircraft to Sprague's assistance.

Taffy 3's carriers meanwhile, adopted a circular formation of about 2,500 yards' diameter. Their escorts, belching smoke, threw themselves at their enormous adversaries in real and simulated torpedo attack.

The Japanese had opened fire at about 30,000 yards and, what with the mass of smoke and the varying courses adopted by Sprague's ships, took some time to get on target. Salvoes were colour-dyed and Sprague himself later referred to the 'horrid beauty' of the mast-high splashes that punctuated the grey-black hedges of smoke. Ominously, the range was closing rapidly and the tattered formation of the enemy ships was allowing them to work round on either flank.

At 0705, for a providential quarter-hour or so, a heavy rain squall enveloped the beleaguered CVEs, giving Sprague the opportunity to make some ground towards the sanctuary of Leyte Gulf itself.

Kurita meanwhile, was greatly troubled by the uncoordinated attentions of seemingly dozens of aircraft, most of which did not bomb but pressed home strafing attacks. In truth, of course, there simply had not been the time to arm them. Amazingly, the Japanese observers were unfamiliar with the distinctive silhouette of a CVE and, still imagining themselves to be faced with the Third Fleet, the ships hesitated to close to lethal range. Sprague's men were surviving thus far through the sheer ferocity of their response.

A scene from the CVE USS *Kitkun Bay* as she prepares to launch her FM-2 Wildcat fighters. In the distance CVE USS *White Plains* makes smoke while a Japanese salvo explodes in the sea. (NARA)

Inevitably, however, the Americans began to take damage. Coming clear of the smoke, the destroyer *Johnston* attacked with torpedoes at only 10,000 yards. She hit the heavy cruiser *Kumano* but was buried in enemy fire. Hit by three 14in and three 6in shells ('Like a puppy being smacked by a truck') the destroyer was wrecked, near dead in the water and firing her remaining guns under local control.

Her fellow destroyers, *Hoel* and *Heermann*, fared similarly, but their 'fierce face' tactics, threatening the enemy with torpedoes that they no longer possessed, caused the Japanese to fragment even further by virtue of individual ships' evasive tactics. Before she sank, the *Hoel* had been struck by about 40 shells of all calibres. Most had passed straight through her.

Visibility, thanks to rain squalls and smoke, now varied between 100 and 25,000 yards. At any glimpse of the carriers, the enemy fired opportunistically, the near misses from heavy-calibre shells racking their light structure.

Pressed hard, Sprague ordered away the four little destroyer escorts, his final line of defence. Designed as AS escorts, the DEs had torpedo tubes but had never used them. Now the ships were ordered to plug the gaps in the smoke and to attack with torpedoes on opportunity. This was learning the hard way. Nimble, they escaped damage for a while by 'chasing salvoes', but there were just too many salvoes. The *Samuel B. Roberts*, which had attached herself to the destroyers, was similarly devastated by 14in projectiles. Over half her crew were killed, missing or died from wounds.

Japanese destroyers tried to work around the flank in order to deliver their own torpedo attack but, frustrated by smoke and under the heavy attention of Taffy 2 aircraft, they were obliged to retire. It was now 0845 and although Kurita had lost all tactical control, the prospects for Sprague looked bleak indeed.

The remaining Japanese cruisers had ordered themselves into a column which overhauled the Americans on their port side, while the destroyers tried again to starboard. Astern were the heavy units with the remainder of the Centre Group.

All Sprague's CVEs were now making their best speed on a south-westerly course direct to the gulf. This meant that all aircraft launch and

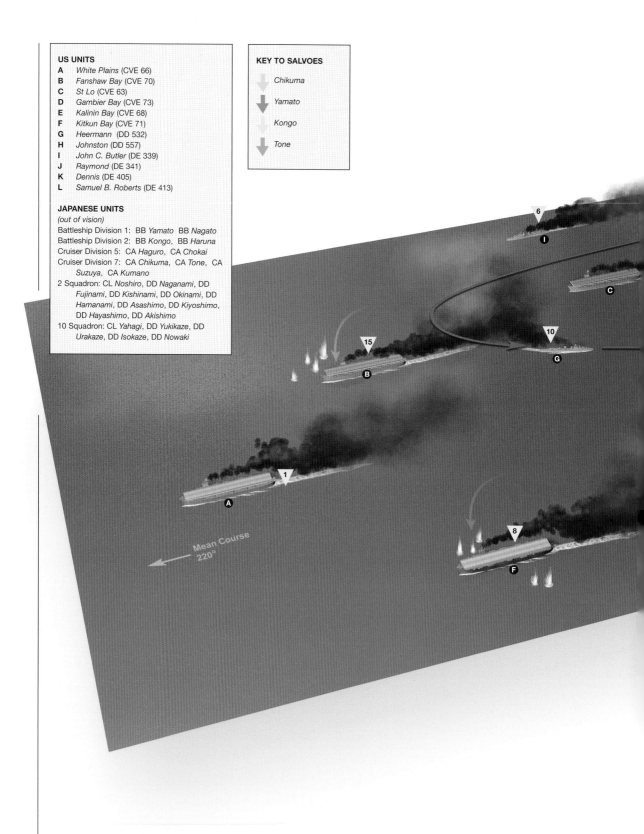

US UNITS
A *White Plains* (CVE 66)
B *Fanshaw Bay* (CVE 70)
C *St Lo* (CVE 63)
D *Gambier Bay* (CVE 73)
E *Kalinin Bay* (CVE 68)
F *Kitkun Bay* (CVE 71)
G *Heermann* (DD 532)
H *Johnston* (DD 557)
I *John C. Butler* (DE 339)
J *Raymond* (DE 341)
K *Dennis* (DE 405)
L *Samuel B. Roberts* (DE 413)

JAPANESE UNITS
(out of vision)
Battleship Division 1: BB *Yamato* BB *Nagato*
Battleship Division 2: BB *Kongo*, BB *Haruna*
Cruiser Division 5: CA *Haguro*, CA *Chokai*
Cruiser Division 7: CA *Chikuma*, CA *Tone*, CA
    Suzuya, CA *Kumano*
2 Squadron: CL *Noshiro*, DD *Naganami*, DD
    Fujinami, DD *Kishinami*, DD *Okinami*, DD
    Hamanami, DD *Asashimo*, DD *Kiyoshimo*,
    DD *Hayashimo*, DD *Akishimo*
10 Squadron: CL *Yahagi*, DD *Yukikaze*, DD
    Urakaze, DD *Isokaze*, DD *Nowaki*

KEY TO SALVOES

Chikuma

Yamato

Kongo

Tone

Mean Course 220°

THE BATTLE OFF SAMAR, 25 OCTOBER 1944 – 0820–0850

Early on 25 October 1944, Kurita's Central Force was heading south to attack Leyte Gulf assault area. At 0645 it sighted Sprague's 'Taffy 3' escort carrier Group to the east of Samar. Surprise was mutual and total. The carriers headed southwest while the US destroyers valiantly strove to hold off the overwhelming Japanese force.

Note: Ships are not to scale

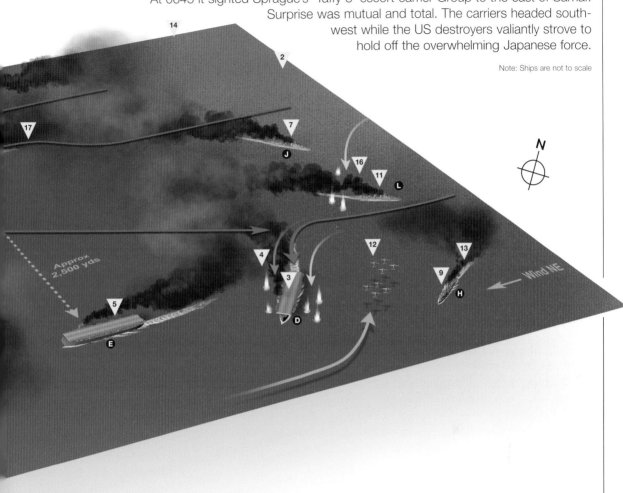

EVENTS

1 0820: Taffy 3 steaming at 17.5 knots on 220°. DD *Johnston* has torpedoed CL *Kumano*, while CL *Suzuya* has fallen out after being severely damaged. Well by bombs. DD *Hoel* has been severely damaged. The Japanese cruiser divisions are gaining on the fleeing escort carriers on both the port and starboard bows, while the battleships are somewhat behind.

2 0820: Japanese battleship Div. 1 fires on escort carriers by radar.

3 0820: Shell from CA *Chikuma* hits CVE *Gambier Bay*.

4 0820: BB *Yamato* fires on CVE *Gambier Bay*. CVE *Gambier Bay* falling behind other escort carriers.

5 0825: CVE *Kalinin Bay* fires on CA *Chikuma* and scores hit.

6 0826: DEs *Dennis* and *Butler*, steaming on the starboard quarter, are ordered to move to port quarter to fend off Japanese cruisers. They are joined later by DE *Raymond*.

Japanese cruisers *Chikuma* and *Tone* are closest, with *Haguro* and *Chokai* behind. US destroyers and destroyer escorts lay smoke to protect the CVEs.

7 0828: DE *Raymond* opens fire on CAs *Chikuma* and *Tone*.

8 0828: 8-inch salvo 1,000 yards astern of CVE *Kitkun Bay*, which zigzags, followed at 0830 by salvo 100 yards off port beam.

9 0830: DD *Johnston* fires on CA *Chikuma*.

10 0835: DD *Heermann* passes behind CVE *Fanshaw Bay*, almost colliding with her. DD *Heermann* almost collides with DD *Johnston* before firing on CA *Chikuma*.

11 0841: DE *Roberts* fires on CA *Chikuma* and knocks out 8-inch turret.

12 0842: Taffy 2 aircraft attack CAs *Chikuma* and *Chokai*.

13 0845: DD *Johnston* engages BB *Kongo*.

14 0847: Japanese 2 Squadron, including CL *Noshiro*, reported closing on starboard quarter while Japanese 10 Squadron begins approach for torpedo attack.

15 0850: CVE *Fanshaw Bay* hit by 6-inch shell from CA *Tone*.

16 0850: DE *Roberts* narrowly missed by 14-inch salvo from BB *Kongo*.

17 CVEs continue to weave and zigzag on mean course.

Japanese cruiser *Chikuma* evades attack during the Battle off Samar. A bomb has already blown off part of her stern. *Chikuma* played a leading role in the battle, focusing much of her attack on the US CVE *Gambier Bay*. (NARA)

recovery was nearly down-wind. Most did not attempt recovery but flew on directly to Taffy 2's decks for re-arming

So close were the enemy cruisers that the CVEs were using their single 5in guns to return fire through gaps in the smoke. With a following wind, Sprague's remaining escorts had difficulty in keeping the formation fully screened with smoke, but rapid course changes kept the enemy gunners unsettled and, for the most part, their salvoes met empty ocean within the general grey gloom.

The heavy projectiles that struck the carriers were armour-piercing and passed straight through without exploding, but 6in and 8in shells were very damaging. The *Kalinin Bay* somehow survived one 14in or 16in hit and no less than 13 of 8in. 'Ziggy' Sprague's flagship, *Fanshaw Bay* took four 8in direct hits and a pair of bone-jarring near misses.

It was, however, the *St. Lo* and *Gambier Bay*, on the quarters of the formation, that took most punishment, being closest and most frequently visible to the enemy. First taken under fire at some 17,000 yards, the *Gambier Bay* found the enemy's salvo corrections to be so predictable that she could successfully dodge them but, by the time that the range had dropped to only 10,000 yards, it was only a matter of time. Although defended heroically by two of the escorts, the carrier took the brunt of the fire of three heavy and one light cruiser. Hit time and again, she came to a halt, blazing and settling.

The enemy was not having it all his own way, however, for, even as the *Gambier Bay* rolled over at 0905, a group of divebombers from the *Kitkun Bay* put a devastatingly accurate attack into the heavy cruiser *Chokai*, which sank in about 20 minutes.

By 0924 the tophamper of the Japanese battleships was visible even from Stump's Taffy 2, close enough also to attract a few ranging salvoes. Stump had already despatched four strikes and, at 0935, sent off a fifth. Many were torpedo armed and, although the Japanese criticised the weapons as being slow and easy to evade, it would seem that, of the 49 expended, between five and 11 found a billet. One casualty was certainly the heavy cruiser *Chikuma*.

Kurita was aware that he, too, was accumulating cripples, notably the *Kumano* by destroyer torpedo, and the *Suzuya*, fatally damaged by bombing. These would hamper any rapid retirement and, worryingly, his totally disordered force was now running into a second carrier group. Although this comprised Stump's CVEs, Japanese battle reports spoke of firing on 'Ranger-class carriers', escorted by 'Baltimore-class cruisers'. Now hardly 50 miles distant from his Leyte objective, Kurita was still convinced that he was battling the Third Fleet. He also reasoned that the delay caused by this opposition would have allowed the Americans to have cleared the gulf of all amphibious shipping and transports. Even if he succeeded in fighting his way through, therefore, he would face certain annihilation for no return. Fatigued by his recent experiences, his resolve wavered.

In truth, there was little more to prevent Kurita from pressing on, clear to the invasion zone, but never was the expression 'the Fog of War' more appropriate. The continuous smoke curtains made optical range-finding difficult (at one point, Sprague was credited by the Japanese with making 30 knots. 'I knew that I was scared' he later said, 'but not that scared!') and Japanese radar was not up to the task.

At 0911 Kurita ordered his scattered units to retire northward and to re-form, and it was with disbelief that Sprague's weary crews saw them pull away. The Japanese commander had also been receiving disquieting signals regarding the fate of the Southern Force (see below) and, reluctant to expend his own formation, yet equally reluctant to retire, a now-unmolested Kurita spent over three hours steering an apparently aimless course off Samar, determining what best to do.

What was certain was that further dalliance would only invite massive American retribution, which could be expected to appear over the horizon at any time. At 1310, Kurita ordered retirement and the surface action off Samar was over.

A Japanese plane plummets towards the sea after being shot down over CVE *Kitkun Bay*. (NARA)

OZAWA'S NORTHERN FORCE

The Battle off Cape Engaño (25 October)

'In case opportunity for destruction of major portions of the enemy fleet offers, or can be created, such destruction becomes the primary task [of all Pacific Ocean Area forces].' So had run the directive passed to Adm Halsey by Adm Nimitz, Commander-in-Chief, US Pacific Fleet. Bearing in mind that:

(i)   Its carriers had been, by far, the most potent arm of the Imperial Japanese Navy,

(ii) He, himself, had considerable experience of naval action, but that

(iii) His distinguished career had never included leading a fleet in major action.

it is perhaps, not surprising that Halsey was so ready to believe that Kurita's Centre Group had been reduced to a state where Kinkaid's Seventh Fleet could easily deal with it, while he invoked his chief's instruction to go after the all-important enemy carriers, i.e. Ozawa's Northern Force. He could scarcely have known, and certainly could never have assumed, that Ozawa's carriers had so few aircraft embarked.

Heading north at easy speed to avoid over-running the enemy by night, Halsey transferred tactical command to V Adm Mitscher who, so often bypassed by his superior, was not best disposed toward him. It has been mentioned already how, once night reconnaissance had established that Kurita was still headed toward the San Bernardino Strait, the task group commanders had signalled their concern to Halsey's flagship, only to be rebuffed.

Mitscher's own flag was worn by the *Lexington*, a carrier of Sherman's TG38.3.

Here, too, there was sufficient consternation to wake the frail admiral in order to appraise him of the developing situation, and to get him to urge Halsey to detach the surface action group, TF34, to cover the strait with all despatch. On being assured that Halsey possessed the same information as his own officers, Mitscher snapped, 'If he wants my advice, he'll ask for it,' and resumed his sleep.

V Adm Lee's Task Force 34 was, therefore, not detached and, by 0430 on 25 October, was leading Mitscher's three carrier groups. Night reconnaissance reports, now some two hours old, had placed Ozawa's force at conflicting distances ahead, and search radar displays were being carefully monitored. On and within the dark masses of the numerous carriers, all was ordered but furious activity to get the initial strikes fully armed and fuelled. Mitscher was not one either to waste time or to be surprised by events.

Preceded by numerous search aircraft, the first strike began to get airborne at 0540. Having gained a specified distance ahead of the fleet, this force had been ordered to orbit until contact with Ozawa was established. This came at 0710. The Japanese were some 200 miles east of Cape Engaño in northern Luzon, just 150 miles from Halsey and, thanks to Mitscher's prescience, only 80 miles from the waiting air strike.

By 0800, therefore, the first Helldivers were plummeting from the high blue to release their deadly loads, while their Hellcat low escort waited to cover them at the vulnerable moment of pulling out. The enemy CAP was barely a dozen strong and, by usual Pacific standards, negligible, and easily dealt with by the upper escort. Evading the dive-bombers put the Japanese formation into disarray, allowing the torpedo-carrying Avengers their chance to select individual targets. Their weapons were released from about 1,500 yards.

The attack was pressed home through heavy anti-aircraft fire. The carrier *Chitose* received a number of bomb hits and was severely shaken by near misses. She lingered a while but was beyond saving, going down at 0937. The carrier *Zuiho* took a single bomb but survived. Wearing Ozawa's flag, and the primary target, the big Pearl Harbor veteran *Zuikaku* was struck by a torpedo near the end of the strike. Listing, slowed and with the communications inoperative, she could no longer function as flagship and Ozawa transferred to the light cruiser *Oyodo*.

As the Japanese no longer had air cover, the Americans were able to station target coordinators to vector-in follow-up strikes, the next of which was airborne a full hour before the return of the first.

This second attack, much smaller, concentrated on the carrier *Chiyoda*. Several bombs set her well ablaze and started progressive flooding. Brought to a standstill, she was being assisted by the hybrid *Hyuga* when the third strike, of a massive 200 aircraft, arrived at about 1310.

Ozawa's undamaged ships were found to be in two main groups, moving at high speed. They had left behind two small groups assisting cripples but, as orders were to disable as many ships as possible, the aviators left the latter for TF34 to finish off by gunfire.

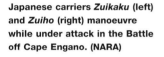

Japanese carriers *Zuikaku* (left) and *Zuiho* (right) manoeuvre while under attack in the Battle off Cape Engano. (NARA)

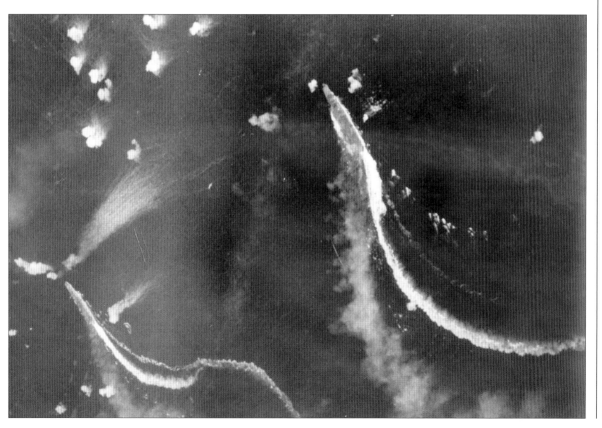

An F6F burns after crash-landing on USS *Enterprise.* A ground crew officer risks severe burns to save the pilot. (NARA)

Vice-Admiral Ozawa transferred his flag from the damaged *Zuikaku* to the light cruiser *Oyodo* on 25 October 1944. This shot is taken from the listing deck of *Zuikaku*. (NARA)

The third strike then concentrated on the already-damaged *Zuikaku,* which still appeared to be full of life. She was caught near-simultaneously by three torpedoes. She staggered, blazing, out of formation, sinking at 1415. Further damaged by bombs, the *Zuiho* continued to survive by virtue of good damage control.

At 1410, to avoid the loss of the *Hyuga* and a destroyer, these were ordered by Ozawa to leave the *Chiyoda* to her fate.

Few American aircraft had been lost and, at 1145, a fourth strike came in. Again, this was only of about 50 aircraft, but these finally put paid to the *Zuiho* before concentrating on the *Hyuga's* sister, *Ise.* Both of these old battleships were tough, however, well-protected and sub-divided, beamy and with serried ranks of automatic weapons. Manoeuvring violently and throwing everything of which she was capable, the *Ise* came through with only a severe shaking.

At 1610 Mitscher ordered away his fifth and largest attack. With the fleets closing, it reached Ozawa's fragmented survivors within the hour.

Admiral Halsey on the bridge of battleship USS *New Jersey*. Halsey was to regret his decision to follow the Japanese carriers north and he was too late to intervene effectively against the marauding Centre Force. (NARA)

The *Ise* and *Hyuga*, now the most attractive targets, received the most attention but, with a superb display of ship handling, suffered no more than near-misses.

As a final gesture, a small sixth strike arrived before 1800. Most of its fliers were now on their third sortie of the day and fatigue meant that the Japanese attracted no further damage.

Ozawa, however, had lost three carriers directly to air attack while the fourth, the abandoned *Chiyoda*, was sunk by gunfire from American cruisers at about 1700. The veteran admiral's feelings at such sacrifice can only be surmised, yet he had not only succeeded totally in his intention to draw off Halsey's Third Fleet but he also brought home the bulk of his remaining force.

For Adm Halsey, 25 October was probably the worst day of his long career. As early as 0725, V Adm McCain's TG38.1, refuelling and still 350 miles distant, picked up the first frantic appeals for assistance from Kinkaid: 'Enemy BB [i.e. battleship] and cruiser reported firing on TU77.4.3 from 15 miles astern'.

Halsey later professed himself baffled as to how Kinkaid and Thomas Sprague had been so taken by surprise, but felt that the combined air power of the three Taffies was sufficient to hold Kurita at bay until Oldendorf could arrive with his half-dozen veteran battleships. This was despite the fact that Kinkaid had been transmitting reports of Oldendorf's participation, well to the south, in the battle against the Japanese Southern Force in the Surigao Strait.

Soon after 0800, Halsey's composure was jolted by a further message: 'Urgently need fast BBs Leyte Gulf at once'. He firmly believed that his role was offensive, not wet-nursing the Seventh Fleet. Ozawa, he later maintained 'greatly threatened not only Kinkaid and myself, but the whole Pacific strategy', which, by any standard, was a considerable exaggeration. Nimitz' original directive had included the explicit instruction that 'Forces of Pacific Ocean Areas will cover and support forces of South-West Pacific', and this Halsey had chosen to ignore.

By now receiving favourable reports of Mitscher's first air strike, Halsey assumed that the lack of aerial opposition was due simply to the Japanese being caught by surprise. Knowing that a second strike was airborne and that Ozawa was already badly hit, Halsey now made what he thought was a considerable gesture. At 0848 he re-directed McCain's TG38.1, the most powerful of his four carrier groups, to proceed from its refuelling 'at best possible speed' to Kinkaid's assistance. For the moment, Lee's TF34 remained heading north.

At about 0900, pressure mounted on an increasingly angry Halsey when Kinkaid signalled: 'Our CVEs being attacked by four BBs, eight cruisers, plus others. Request Lee [i.e. TF34] cover Leyte at top speed. Request fast carriers make immediate strike'.

Several more messages, each more specific, flew directly between the two commanders: no coding and re-transmission delays now. These culminated in Halsey stating that TF38 was engaged with the enemy nearly 400 miles distant north of Leyte Gulf, i.e. too distant to be of any immediate assistance.

Around 1000 Kinkaid appealed again: 'My situation is critical. Fast BBs and support by air strikes may be able to keep enemy from destroying CVEs and entering Leyte'. If Halsey was dismayed by this, he

KAMIKAZE ATTACK ON CVE *KITKUN BAY,* 25 OCTOBER 1944 (pages 70–71)

Although there had been precedents for damaged Japanese aircraft deliberately crashing the ships that they had been targeting, the first instances with encounters with units trained specifically for suicide missions occurred during and after the battle off Samar. The escort carrier (CVE) group of R Adm Clifton A.F. 'Ziggy' Sprague, codenamed Taffy 3, had borne the brunt of the surface gunfire encounter with the enemy and had lost the CVE *Gambier Bay* and three escorts in a desperate action. At 0740, even as Taffy 3 was engaged in fierce surface action, ships of R Adm T.L. 'Tommy' Sprague's Taffy 1, some 130 miles distant, were deliberately dived by six locally based enemy aircraft. One each hit the *Santee* and *Suwannee*, which both survived. By 1040, when Kurita had already pulled away to the north, the mauled Taffy 3 was gratefully retiring to the south when it was targeted by five enemy aircraft which again sought to crash themselves. Only two were successful, one hitting the St Lo, starting fires that eventually brought about her destruction.

The other went for the CVE *Kitkun Bay*, as illustrated here. According to the official history, '*Kitkun Bay*, Admiral Ofstie's flagship, caught the first attack. A Zeke, crossing her bow from port to starboard, climbed rapidly, rolled and dove [sic] directly at the bridge, strafing. It missed the bridge, passed over the island, crashed the port catwalk and bounced into the sea, but the bomb that it carried exploded, causing considerable damage ...' The Mitsubishi A6M Type O (1), known as either a 'Zeke' or a 'Zero', is carrying a centreline fuel drop tank (2) and a 50kg bomb (3) under the port wing. *Kitkun Bay* belonged to the 50-strong Casablanca class and her box-like island structure has an open bridge protected by the sun by a light metal canopy (4). The forward elevator (5) is nearly opposite the bridge. Abaft the elevator are the barrier pendants of the arrester system. The guns are 20mm Oerlikons (6). The flight deck is covered with transversely laid wooden planks, interspersed about every two metres with a perforated steel strip (7) to facilitate drainage and provide securing points for aircraft. The ship had four unusually shaped funnels (8). *Kitkun Bay* carried types SK, SG and YE radars and antennae (9).

Grumman F6F 3 Hellcat fighters, with folding wings. Task Force 38 had almost 550 of these fighters, which were more than a match for the Japanese Zero and which ensured US aerial supremacy over Leyte. (NARA)

was almost immediately galvanized by a signal from Nimitz himself from Pearl Harbor: 'Turkey trots to water GG Where is repeat where is Task Force Thirty Four RR The World wonders'. The signal was copied to both King and Kinkaid.

On, mistakenly, being handed the complete text, Halsey was incoherent with rage. In truth, Nimitz had simply asked 'Where *is* TF34?' His staff officers had added the 'repeat' and the further addressees, while the communicator had attached the routine and meaningless padding at either end of the message to confuse enemy cryptographers. Reading the complete text, however, Halsey interpreted it as CinC signalling with heavy irony and inviting others to be party to the fact.

Probably never more furious in his short-fused existence, the admiral now had to face the reality of the situation. With the beaten and scattered remnants of the enemy's Northern Force just 40 miles from his 16in guns and the action that he so desired, Halsey divided his forces. Ordering Sherman and Davison to finish off Ozawa, he put about both TF34's battleships and Bogan's TG.38.2 for Leyte Gulf. The time was 1055.

HALSEY'S THIRD FLEET

The Run to the South (25 October)

As Halsey knew and had exhaustively explained, taking TF34 and a carrier group south was simply a waste of resources. Astern of him was a fragmented Japanese Northern Force, ripe for annihilation, while now, at 1115, the chaotic encounter east of Samar was already over. Although Kurita still hovered, menacingly but indecisively, Taffy 3's survivors were gratefully closing the safety of the gulf.

Lee's big guns could not reach the San Bernardino Strait before 0100 on the following morning. Kurita could retire through it long before this

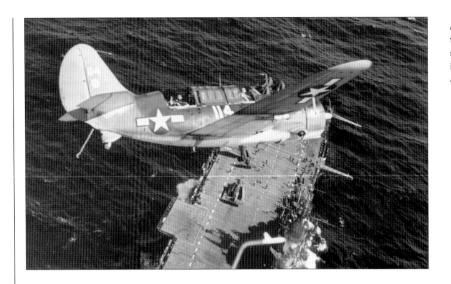

and only air strikes could stop him. But air strikes from where? Bogan's
TG38.2, with Halsey, was too far to the north. McCain's TG38.1 was
beyond effective range to the east. The Taffies, having chalked-up a
notable success, had lost about 50 aircraft and were exhausted. Land-
based air attack was not yet feasible because the only occupied airfield, at
Tacloban, was waterlogged and not really operative, despite a huge effort.

Frustratingly, Halsey could not even work up to full speed. Having
ordered a destroyer screen to accompany him southward, he now
discovered them to be low on fuel. About two-and-a-half hours had to be
spent proceeding at 12 knots as the little ships were partially topped up
from the battleships.

Halsey was now in a dreadful limbo. There were enemies to the north
and enemies to the south. Both, for different reasons, were beyond
reach. The long barrels of his 16in guns, instead of dealing retribution,
pointed mutely at miles of uninterrupted blue ocean.

Divine Wind

For nearly two hours after Halsey turned his heavy forces southward,
Kurita's Centre Group hovered menacingly while its admiral prevaricated.
Taffy 3 had slipped away but, unfortunately, this did not mean the end of
the escort carriers' ordeal, for Thomas Sprague's Taffy 1 was facing its own
challenge.

Most southern of the three CVE groups, Taffy 1 had sent off a 28-plane
strike at daybreak, directed at the Japanese Southern Force. Within the
hour it was despatching every other available aircraft to the assistance of
Taffy 3. In the midst of all this furious activity, nobody had time to consider
the near non-existent threat from enemy land-based aircraft.

It was still early in the action when, at 0740, six Japanese aircraft
appeared from the direction of Mindanao. From a patch of cloud, one
dived on the *Santee*. To those manning the ship's automatic weapons, it
looked like an orthodox bombing run but, firing its guns in one long
continuous burst, it made no attempt to pull out. Passing straight
through the flight deck, port side forward, the aircraft exploded in the
hangar space. The *Santee* was fortunate for, despite fierce localized fires,
nearby ordnance burned without exploding.

Misfortunes rarely come singly, however, and, in the midst of this crisis, the ship was struck by a submarine torpedo. It was a timely reminder that other foes were lurking but, although out of the fight, the *Santee*, survived. Converted from a tanker, she was saved by her excellent sub-division, which contained the flooding.

Two others of the marauders had been shot down by the *Suwannee* when a third, despite damage, deliberately crashed her, well aft. Again, the ship survived fire and explosion, but was severely incapacitated.

Enemy aircraft, usually *in extremis*, had crashed ships on earlier occasions, but such incidents had been isolated and by decision of individual pilots. The morning of 25 October 1944, however, saw the first deployment of the new corps of Kamikaze ('Divine Wind'), units piloted by men prepared to sacrifice themselves in disciplined, premeditated attack. Their bomb and fuel-laden aircraft became, literally, guided missiles whose guidance system was human.

As Taffy 1 cleared its debris and tended the injured, it was Clifton Sprague's Taffy 3 that was singled out for further punishment. Obviously following a rehearsed routine, five enemy aircraft came in very low, below radar level. Short of their chosen objectives, and while the Americans were yet reacting, they suddenly climbed rapidly and dived from about 5,000 feet.

One grazed the *Kitkun Bay*, causing topside damage as its bomb exploded. Two more selected *Fanshaw Bay*, but both were shot down. The final pair went for the *White Plains*. One was destroyed just short of its target but the second, seemingly deterred by the volume of fire, veered off course and struck the neighbouring *St. Lo*. Penetrating again to the hangar deck before exploding, the aircraft initiated a train of detonations that tore the ship apart. Struck at 1050, her gutted wreck disappeared at 1125. This new form of attack had serious implications for the whole US surface fleet.

KURITA'S CENTRE GROUP

Kurita's Deliverance (25–26 October)

While Kurita agonized as to whether he should retire, he was hit at 1220 by a final ragged strike mounted by Taffies 2 and 3. Savaged by surface gunfire and by kamikaze attack, the CVE groups were still full of fight.

Far to the east V Adm McCain had been receiving the anguished calls for assistance from Kinkaid and Thomas Sprague. At 0848 came the direct instruction from Halsey to cease fuelling and to assist however possible. TG38.1 re-formed immediately and worked up 30 knots toward the sound of the guns. By 1040, in one of the most distant carrier strikes of the war, his ships had launched 100 aircraft from a range of 335 miles. Due to the need for maximum fuel, only bombs, no torpedoes, could be carried.

Vectored-in by Taffy 2's flagship, *Natoma Bay*, the attack developed at 1315. Like the Taffies' final efforts, slowed by fatigue, McCain's aircraft caused little damage to Kurita, several of whose ships were trailing oil.

Meanwhile, however, Kurita and Halsey were steering near-opposite courses and were closing rapidly. The indispensable night-fliers of the *Independence* again established first contact, actually sighting the enemy Centre Group as, at 2140, it entered the San Bernardino Strait in single

column. Halsey ordered both carrier groups to be ready at daybreak, in order to 'kick the hell' out of the retreating Japanese.

Fearing the obvious, that Kurita would beat him to the strait, Halsey had formed a chase squadron of his fastest ships, led by his own *New Jersey*. This, TG34.5, was, ironically, a further mistake for, had it pushed ahead of Bogan's air cover and successfully intercepted Kurita, it would have found itself inadequate to defeat him. Fortunately, it arrived at the entrance to the San Bernardino about three hours late and, sweeping on down the coast of Samar, was able to catch only the destroyer *Nowake*, left behind to rescue survivors.

Having rendezvoused at about 0500 on the 26th, the two carrier groups began launching a first strike an hour later. The Japanese were not located, however, until 0810, when a second strike was despatched. A third left at 1245. To these three waves, totalling 257 sorties, was added for good measure an attack by 47 Army B-24s flying from Morotai.

Weariness had now blunted the attack, however, and Kurita was fortunate in losing only the light cruiser *Noshiro* and a destroyer. The heavy cruiser *Kumano*, already lacking her bow, was further damaged but survived.

So far as Leyte Gulf was concerned, Kurita's Centre Group had left the stage. Faltering leadership had seen it fail to achieve its mission and the successful extrication of a large proportion of the force counted for little as all had been ordered to sacrifice themselves if need be to destroy the American amphibious fleet.

THE SOUTHERN FORCE

The Approach Phase (24 October)

In following the fortunes of the Japanese Centre and Northern forces it has been necessary, to avoid confusion, to ignore the progress and the

Dramatic action in Ormoc Bay as the bow of a Japanese destroyer is blown off in an attack by US B-25 Mitchell bombers. (Sea bird Publishing Inc Collection)

fate of the Southern Fleet. It will be recalled that this was to comprise the Van Group of V Adm Nishimura and the Rear Group of V Adm Shima, of these, the former was the larger, consisting of the veteran battleships *Yamashiro* (flag) and *Fuso*, the heavy cruiser *Mogami* and four destroyers. In the rear were the heavy cruisers *Nachi* (flag) and *Ashigara*, the light cruiser *Abukuma* and seven destroyers.

Reference to Map 3 on page 27 shows how Nishimura, having separated from Kurita at Brunei Bay, followed a course up the eastern side of Palawan before crossing the open space of the Sulu Sea. Shima, having left Japan a week earlier, had passed through the Formosa Strait before heading southward. His force entered the Sulu Sea from the north and approached that of Nishimura near the island of Negros.

From the diagram on page 20 it can be seen that Shima and Nishimura were in separate command chains. Although they were intended to work together as the southern pincer of the coordinated attack on Leyte Gulf, and Shima had been ordered to 'support and cooperate' with Nishimura, neither had been given instructions with respect to joint action. Shima was the more senior and, although there is no evidence of previous hostility between the two, he possibly resented the fact that he had not been formally declared leader of a combined Southern Force. Nishimura, for his part, a proven sea officer, was probably unhappy at the prospect of being subordinate to Shima, who had risen to flag rank through staff appointments. As it was, neither attempted to communicate with the other. The Southern Force, therefore, was effectively two separate squadrons, working independently under different senior officers. It demonstrated an inexcusable lack of initiative in officers so senior, suggesting an offended *amour-propre*.

Having made detours to avoid the suspected locations of American submarines, Nishimura's Van Group made steady and uneventful progress until 0905 on 24 October, when search aircraft from Davison's TG38.4 reported it to be about 50 miles west of the most southerly point of Negros. Shima's Rear Group was sighted some three hours later by a B-24 of the Fifth Army Air Force, which observed it near the Cagayan Islands and steering south-eastward, also to round Negros.

Davison's search aircraft were, in fact, a 28-strong formation, many of which were armed with bombs. Having reported Nishimura, they attacked. As usual, the results were considerably over-stated, being limited to a bomb on the *Fuso*'s quarterdeck and damage to a destroyer. Neither was significantly damaged.

Reported again at about 1240, Nishimura then went unobserved for nearly 12 hours because Davison's task group, as the others, had been ordered north by Halsey. On advising the latter that his aircraft were tracking a substantial Japanese force, Davison was told that the Seventh Fleet had adequate resources to deal with it. This was despite the sighting reports so far being contradictory with respect to ship numbers and types. The result, however, was that Kinkaid's main firepower was drawn south to deal with the Southern Force at a time when it would be urgently needed off Samar to deal with Kurita's Centre Group.

For his part, Kinkaid was content enough to take on the Southern Force and conferred at length with his staff. His intelligence officer had accurately estimated that Nishimura was headed for Leyte Gulf via the Surigao Strait and that his attack would be timed for dawn on the 25th. At a time when Kinkaid needed regular reports of the enemy's progress, the support of Davison was removed. The Seventh Fleet Commander was thus reliant upon radar-equipped PBYs, which failed to find the Japanese at all.

KINKAID'S SEVENTH FLEET

Kinkaid's dispositions (24 October)

For the purpose of supporting the invasion of the Philippines, Adm Nimitz had temporarily transferred considerable assets from the Pacific Fleet to the Seventh Fleet. To provide the heavy and sustained gun support that was so important a feature of landings, Kinkaid had been lent no less than six battleships. All were old, the newest launched in 1921. Five had been at Pearl Harbor, during which raid two of them had been sunk, later to be raised and refitted. Although capable of barely 20 knots, however, all had tough hides and, between them, mounted 16 16in and 48 14in guns.

The six had been operating in two groups of three, designated Fire Support Units, North and South. Now faced with the threat of the Japanese Southern Force, they would be employed as originally intended, as a battle line to defeat an enemy in a surface gun action.

There was a problem in that their magazines had been loaded three-quarters with high-capacity (HC) rounds, better suited to shore bombardment than the armour-piercing (AP) shells necessary to knock out a battleship opponent. They had, in addition, already fired off a proportion of their ammunition in their intended role. None had less than

200 AP rounds aboard, however, and that would need to suffice, for there was precious little time to load more from what small stocks were available.

Early in the afternoon of the 24th Kinkaid alerted all units to the strong likelihood of an enemy attack during the coming night, and charged R Adm Jesse B. Oldendorf, overall commander of the bombardment groups, to plan the necessary Seventh Fleet dispositions to meet it. The very experienced Oldendorf had already been devoting considerable thought to the matter and, as he explained later, worked on the theory of the old-time gambler: 'Never give a sucker a chance. If my opponent is foolish enough to come at me with an inferior force, I'm certainly not going to give him an even break'.

A primary concern was for the mass of mercantile shipping laying in the gulf and carrying *matériel* for the forces ashore. These were effectively corralled and, with the three vital but unarmed amphibious force flagships, were ringed by escorts. All ship movement was ordered to cease at dusk.

Map 6 on page 82 shows clearly how Oldendorf then turned geography to his advantage. Once exiting the wide spaces of the Sulu Sea, the enemy would have to pass between Negros and Mindanao to enter the more constricted Mindanao Sea. His approach was then constricted at Panaon Island before he turned northward, up the Surigao Strait. What the Japanese had hoped would be an unobtrusive route to Leyte Gulf, Oldendorf then turned into a blind alley.

Shorelines, for the most part, were steep and heavily wooded. By night, when the enemy would make his approach, small combatants would visually disappear against this backdrop, which would also act to confuse radar returns. Among his various naval assets, Kinkaid could count 39 PT boats (called Motor Torpedo Boats by the British). Now lacking effective night-flying reconnaissance aircraft, Oldendorf organized the craft in 13 three-boat sections and stationed them over the 100 miles or so between Bohol Island and Surigao Strait. Their task was to lay silently, report the passage of the enemy and then to attack, section by section.

As Halsey was assumed to be controlling the northern approaches to Leyte Gulf, a maximum number of surface combatants were used in Oldendorf's planned deployments. Twenty-eight destroyers (one of them Australian) would ambush the Japanese in the strait itself. This averaged a useful 15 miles or so in width but, being irregular, would

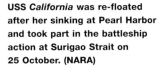

USS *California* was re-floated after her sinking at Pearl Harbor and took part in the battleship action at Surigao Strait on 25 October. (NARA)

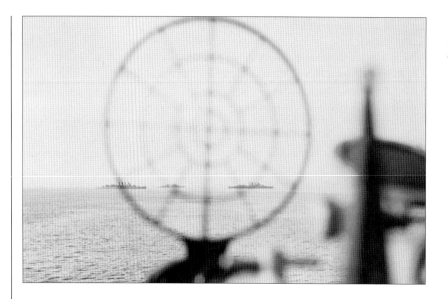

The Australian cruisers HMAS *Shropshire* (left) and HMAS *Australia* (right) took part at Leyte Gulf, with *Shropshire* present in the cruiser line at Surigao Strait. (NARA)

oblige the enemy almost certainly to follow a median course. Keeping close under the coasts the destroyers, organized in divisions, would sweep down the strait on either side, in the direction of the advancing enemy. On sighting him, the divisions would turn 180 degrees, release torpedoes and retire northward at high speed in the direction from which they had come.

Those Japanese ships that had survived the attacks so far would then be approaching the upper end of the strait, only to find Oldendorf's heavy units disposed across their path, blocking the exit to the gulf itself. The six battleships (placed under the tactical command of R Adm George L. Weyler) would steam in open water and in battle line, allowing their full broadside to be brought to bear in unobstructed fire. Their limited outfit of AP ammunition would be fired off first and, to ensure maximum effect, Weyler was ordered to hold his fire until the range had dropped to 20,000 yards. The Japanese would be at a grave disadvantage for, although the Americans would have 64 heavy guns bearing at once, their two battleships would be approaching head-on, so that, even if one ship was not obstructing the fire of the other, the maximum that they could deploy would be just eight barrels.

Nor was this the sum total of the forces arrayed against the enemy. On the flanks of Weyler's battle line, plugging the gaps between its extremities and the neighbouring shorelines, cruiser forces were deployed. On the left, under Oldendorf himself, were three heavy and two light cruisers. On the right were one heavy (Australian) cruiser and two light, under the tactical control of the American R Adm Russell S. Berkey.

The action, seemingly inevitable, would be fought in darkness, with neither side able to employ aircraft. It would be the last example of such.

THE SOUTHERN FORCE

Battle of Surigao Strait. Phase I (24–25 October)
Their engines cut, the PT boats waited, silently and apprehensively. It was hot, it was humid, the strait lit faintly by a quarter moon that was a

little over an hour from setting when, at 2236, PT-131 of Section One, laying off Bohol, detected Nishimura's Van Group on radar. The heavy silence of the tropic night was shattered as the three-boat section started engines and wound-on revolutions for 24 knots.

At this point, the *Mogami* and three destroyers had been sent ahead, the two battleships and a single destroyer, *Shigure*, trailing. The latter ships, threatened from their starboard side, turned towards their assailants. Immediately, the PT boats were in desperate action as the *Shigure* fixed them by searchlight and engaged them with all available weapons. PTs 130 and 152 were hit, the former making smoke to shield her colleague and to cover her own retirement, for no contact report had yet been made. Without her radio, the PT had to approach Section Two on the opposite side of the strait. It was thus from here that PT-127 first raised the alarm at 0010. R Adm Oldendorf received the message a quarter-hour later; gratefully, for it was the first accurate indication of the Southern Force's position for over 14 hours.

As was too often the case with light forces, the PTs had received very little exercise in torpedo attack. Since their arrival, they had been employed on myriad useful tasks but, as a result, lacked the experience that only constant exercise and exposure to action can confer. Section One's failure to report before attacking was compounded by its being unable to achieve a favourable attacking position under a barrage of fire from the *Shigure*.

Although Nishimura had received the signal from Kurita, warning that the Centre Group had been delayed and could not attack before 1100 on the following morning, he pushed on at 18 knots. Shima, in the rear, was actually 40 miles adrift when Nishimura first reported that he was repelling PT boats. The Rear Group was then in a column of three cruisers, led by a pair of destroyers abreast, acting as scouts. The remaining destroyers flanked the cruisers.

Section Three fared no better than its colleagues. It attacked the *Mogami* group, but the Japanese demonstrated their recognized aptitude for night-fighting. Searchlights dazzled, illuminated and disorientated the attackers as they tried to negotiate the barrier of medium calibre and automatic fire. All three PT boats were beaten back but, although they survived without major hurt, they had launched only two torpedoes, and these to no effect. Although this skirmish had begun at 2350, it was 0330 before their contact report was despatched.

Reassured by this successful defence and progress to date, Nishimura signalled at 0100 to Kurita (whose Centre Group had already exited the San Bernardino) and to Shima, that he would pass Panaon Island, and thus enter the Surigao Strait, at 0130. For this final approach, he closed up his formation. Two destroyers probed ahead, followed at about 4,000 yards by the flagship *Yamashiro*, herself flanked by the remaining two destroyers. Astern, stationed at 1,000-yard intervals, followed the *Fuso* and *Mogami*.

Five more PT sections were waiting in the eight-mile gap between Panaon and Mindanao. The moon had now set and an overcast sky brought occasional little rain squalls down the ink-black strait. At this point the Japanese were vulnerable as they made a six-point alteration in course to take them into the strait proper. Their defence was as alert and effective as ever, and the small American craft were again brushed

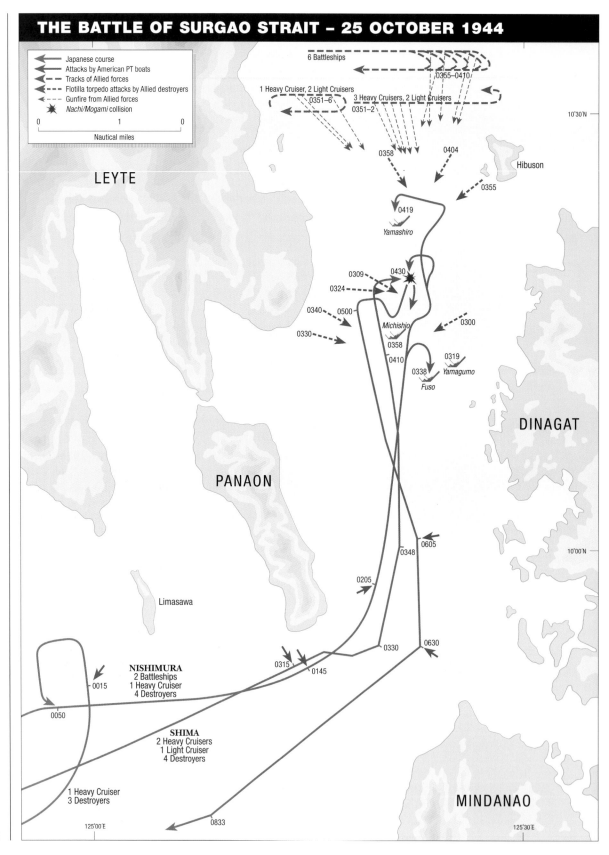

Japanese course
Attacks by American PT boats
Tracks of Allied forces
Flotilla torpedo attacks by Allied destroyers
Gunfire from Allied forces
Nachi/Mogami collision

0   1   0
Nautical miles

6 Battleships

1 Heavy Cruiser, 2 Light Cruisers
0351–6

3 Heavy Cruisers, 2 Light Cruisers
0351–2

0355–0410

10°30′N

LEYTE

0358

0404

Hibuson

0355

0419

Yamashiro

0309
0324
0340
0500
0330

0430

0300

Michishio
0358
0410
0338
0319
Yamagumo
Fuso

DINAGAT

PANAON

10°00′N

0605
0348

0205

Limasawa

0330
0630

0315
0145

NISHIMURA
2 Battleships
1 Heavy Cruiser
4 Destroyers

0015

0050

SHIMA
2 Heavy Cruisers
1 Light Cruiser
4 Destroyers

1 Heavy Cruiser
3 Destroyers

MINDANAO

0833

125°00′E

125°30′E

aside. One, PT-493, was destroyed outright by three 4.7in hits from an escorting destroyer.

At 0213 the Van Group successfully fought off the last of the light craft. Three further sections of PTs lay ahead, but these were ordered to stay clear to enable the destroyers to commence their attacks.

The failure of the PT boats would have been complete had they not also attacked Shima's Rear Group. This force was rounding Panaon at about 0325 when PT-137 succeeded in putting a single torpedo into the light cruiser *Abukuma*. She fell out of line and remained afloat, only to be sunk the following day by US Army bombers.

Thirty PTs had seen action, firing a total of 34 torpedoes for one hit. Ten boats had been damaged by return fire, one of them sinking. Could the destroyers fare any better?

Battle of Surigao Strait. Phase II (25 October)

Some 10,000 yards south of Weyler's battleships, Destroyer Squadron 54 (Desron 54) was likewise patrolling laterally across the northern end of the Surigao Strait. While still awaiting news that the enemy's Southern Force was approaching, the squadron was divided into three sections by its senior officer, Capt Jesse B. Coward. Two ships were moved a little north to maintain a picket, while the remaining five comprised a section of three (*McGowan, Melvin* and *Remey* under Coward himself) to patrol the eastern half of the legs, and a pair (*McDermut* and *Monssen* under Cdr Richard H. Phillips) to cover the western half.

As reports on Nishimura's progress were then received from the PTs, Oldendorf forwarded them to the destroyermen. By 0200 on the 25th the enemy was distant some 30 miles and Coward decided to move, his division turning southward about ten minutes before that of Phillips.

Coward's orders to his ships were to attack with torpedoes only, with no use of guns to betray their positions. Having delivered its attack, each division was to turn towards the shoreline in order to remain concealed and also to keep the range clear for Weyler's battleships when they opened fire.

At 0240, second-in-line *McGowan* reported a radar contact, fine to starboard, range 18 miles. The two sides were closing at a relative speed of 40 knots, and within five minutes the plot had resolved the contact into a formation of seven ships, three large and four small. At 0250 Coward turned his division two points to port in order to open the firing angle and designated specific targets for each ship of the squadron.

Occasional lightning flickered across the strait as the waiting crews closed up, nerves taut, peering into the blackness ahead. Suddenly, at 0258, there they were, slightly darker masses, as yet indistinct. The range was under 13,000 yards and closing rapidly.

Having enjoyed a quiet half-hour since the last PT-boat attack, the Japanese had, none the less, remained vigilant, and saw this new developing danger. As Coward's division at 0300 swung hard left in sequence to release their torpedoes, the night was, once again, lanced by Japanese searchlights. At 9,000 yards, however, these failed to illuminate the destroyers. The division having fired 27 torpedoes, they made smoke and headed back up the strait at 35 knots under sporadic, but ill-directed, fire. On a medium speed setting, the torpedoes had about eight minutes to run.

Fletcher-class destroyer USS *Monssen* took part in the highly successful destroyer torpedo offensive against Japanese units at Surigao Strait, 24–25 October. (NARA)

Running down the opposite side of the strait somewhat later, Cdr Phillips' division first made radar contact at 0254. He changed course to one more nearly opposite to that of the Japanese. Then, at 0308, he brought the two destroyers hard left, heading almost directly at the enemy who, thoroughly alert, brought the American ships under a heavy and accurate fire. Releasing their torpedoes at 0309, the pair completed their turn and, likewise, retired back up the strait at high speed.

Shortly before Phillips' division fired, several heavy explosions were heard from the direction of the Japanese formation, and the battleship *Fuso* was seen to fall out of line. The hits were credited to the *Melvin*.

Alive to the torpedo danger, Nishimura ordered an emergency eight-point turn to starboard, then another to port to bring him back onto his original course. It availed him nothing as, one by one, the *Yamashiro* and three destroyers were struck. The battleship shrugged off the blow and ploughed on but, of her escorts, the *Yamagumo* sank immediately, the *Michishio* came to a standstill and the *Asagumo* lost her bows, although she was able to make sufficient slow progress to retire.

In an all too rare example of a nocturnal destroyer torpedo attack, Coward's divisions had scored brilliantly. As they pulled out under an unpleasantly hot fire, the *Fuso* was already showing signs of distress.

Now it was the turn of the Desron 24, the six destroyers covering Oldendorf's right flank cruisers. These proceeded down the western side of the strait, organized in two divisions. Their arrival was nicely timed to take advantage of the confusion caused by Coward's squadron.

First in action were the *Killen* and *Beale*, led by the Australian destroyer *Arunta*. Between 0323 and 0326 these loosed 14 torpedoes but, with the Japanese manoeuvring evasively, only one hit was scored, this on the *Yamashiro*.

The other division, headed by Desron 24's senior officer, Capt K.M. McManes, in the *Hutchins*, proceeded further south before launching 15 torpedoes at ranges between 8,000 and 11,000 yards. Unlike Coward's ships, they also used their gun armament, attracting considerable attention in return. Their only success appears to have been to finish off the unfortunate *Michishio*, although, while retiring, they had an excellent view of the *Fuso* exploding into two halves. These drifted down the strait, burning uncontrollably.

At this stage, the badly damaged *Yamashiro* was slowed, but still on course. On her starboard quarter was the as yet undamaged *Mogami* and just one surviving destroyer, *Shigure*. Their ordeal by torpedo was not yet over, however, as the nine left-flank destroyers were now unleashed. Of these, two sections of three approached the enemy from his starboard bow while the third section, under their senior officer, Capt Roland N. Smoot, came from his port. The former group fired a total of 30 torpedoes between 0354 and 0359 but, despite the short range of 8,000 yards, all missed. A contributory factor to this poor result was that Weyler's battle line had already opened fire.

Capt Smoot left it a little late, not firing until 0414. One of his ships, the *Newcomb*, claimed to have hit a battleship with one, possibly two, torpedoes. Both sides, however, were now exchanging fire at maximum rate and the centre of the strait was a very dangerous place to be. Before Smoot could disengage, his tail-ender, *Grant*, came under a deluge of fire from both sides. Her 18 hits were subsequently identified as 11 from an American light cruiser and seven from Japanese medium-calibre weapons. She was extricated only with great difficulty and, of all the destroyers engaged, was the only one to sustain casualties – 34 dead and missing, 94 wounded. Despite this setback, the destroyers had performed magnificently, making some of the most effective attacks of the naval war.

Battle of Surigao Strait. Phase III (25 October)

As the destroyers dealt out death to the stubbornly advancing Japanese, Oldendorf's force of battleships and cruisers silently marked time in their columns across the head of the strait, their fire-control teams (or, at least those with up-to-date radars) studying the enemy's progress as a cat watches the movement of a creature in the grass. The balance of hitting power was now so weighted against the Japanese that their situation was utterly hopeless. Each of the Allied ships had a perfectly clear line of fire, and the situation was developing as in a textbook diagram.

Oldendorf himself was aboard the *Louisville*, lead cruiser of the left-flank force. At 0351, while the destroyers were still engaged, he ordered left and right-flank cruisers to open fire. Some of the ships were of pre-war build, mounting 15 6in guns; later cruisers had 12. All fired at prodigious rates, their full broadsides erupting at 15-second intervals. The newer, 12-gun *Columbia*, for instance, is credited as firing no less than 1,147 rounds in 18 minutes.

Two minutes after the cruisers, the battleships joined in, although the disproportionate advantage of six to one was reduced by the fact that only three of the six had adequate fire control radar. *West Virginia*, *Tennessee* and *California* thus between them, loosed 225 rounds of main battery ammunition while the *Maryland* waited until 0359 before firing. At this point the wall of splashes around the target had grown so massive that *Maryland*'s older radar was able to register on it at some 20,000 yards, enabling her to add six full broadsides of 16in. The *Tennessee* did not fire at all, earning a subsequent censure from her divisional commander. The *Mississippi* was also unable to participate in the main engagement, which terminated at 0409. Then, as Oldendorf ordered a cease-fire and a 16-point turn together, the *Mississippi* suddenly acquired a large target and fired her only broadside of the battle.

Nishimura has to be credited with raw courage as he gamely led his already tattered squadron into this inferno, a continuous hail of projectiles whose tracer trails were described by Capt Smoot (who was all too close) as being 'like a continual [sic] stream of lighted railroad cars going over a hill'.

Neither of the two larger Japanese warships had useful fire-control radar and, as the Americans were using flashless propellant, they made poor visual targets. The stricken *Yamashiro* appeared to be engaging the tail of the left-flank cruisers with her main battery and the retiring destroyers with her secondary armament. Both she and the *Mogami*, however, were being smothered in hits of all calibres from 6in to 16in. It was beyond the power of any damage control team to keep pace with destruction incurred at this rate.

By 0400 the *Yamashiro* could be seen on fire at so many locations that her every detail was clear-cut. If she was still returning fire, nobody noticed it. Her progress checked, she hauled around to port, remained on a near-westerly course for about ten minutes then, still making about 15 knots, turned southward. Flooding uncontrollably, she slowly rolled over and, at 0419, went down, taking with her V Adm Nishimura and the majority of his crew.

If the punishment absorbed by the enemy flagship aroused a grudging admiration on the part of her tormentors, the same was equally true of the *Mogami*. Although the *Yamashiro* attracted the greater proportion of the fire, there was more than enough for both, while the lighter construction of the cruiser was less able to tolerate it. At 0353, seven minutes or so before her flagship, she commenced a port turn which continued through 270 degrees. At 0401, while her heading was approximately southward, she fired torpedoes, probably at Smoot's destroyers, which constituted the most immediate threat. These were observed and reported by the destroyers at 0413, by which time the battle line had checked its fire.

Mogami was now well on fire, her commanding officer and bridge personnel all dead, her machinery spaces damaged. Slowed, she was now heading approximately eastward, shrouded in her own smoke. The respect for Japanese torpedoes was such that, on the report of their running, the battle line turned away in its two divisions. In this there was a faint echo of Jutland and, indeed, the result was similar, for contact with the *Mogami* was not re-established, it being assumed that she, too, had sunk.

The lone Japanese destroyer *Shigure*, led a charmed life that night. In the storm of fire enveloping the bigger ships, she was of little assistance but she was fortunate in taking only one hit, that right aft. Recognizing the hopelessness of the situation and no longer in radio contact with anybody, her commanding officer decided on his own initiative to retire. His flagship was sunk and the *Mogami* appeared doomed so, heading back down the strait, the *Shigure* passed the still-blazing stern portion of the *Fuso* and gratefully gained the relative safety of darkness.

At this point her steering, damaged by the shell hit, failed. Coming to a halt, the *Shigure* drifted silently as her engineers tackled the repair. Then, heart-stoppingly, the dark shapes of large warships loomed from the blackness to the south. The leading ship challenged the *Shigure*, to whose intense relief she identified herself as the *Nachi*. She was at the head of Shima's Rear Group.

Some 40 miles astern of Nishimura at the outset of the action, Shima had been closely following the former's fortunes through monitoring radio transmissions. He had been untroubled until 0325, when his only light cruiser, *Abukuma*, had taken a torpedo from a PT boat and had fallen out.

Heading up the strait with two heavy cruisers and four destroyers, Shima passed the two burning halves of the *Fuso* at 0410. These were assumed to be two separate ships. Ranged ahead, his destroyers reported that all was quiet. Nerves were jittery, for the intense darkness of the night was compounded by the persistent hanging smoke left by the Allied destroyers in covering their retreat.

On his somewhat primitive radar, Shima then detected two large objects ahead, distant some 13,000 yards. He ordered his cruisers to fire torpedoes. At 0424, therefore, both turned eight points to starboard and launched eight weapons apiece. The 'targets', however, remain a mystery, for there were no islands there and no ship was ever hit.

The 90-degree turn then became one of 180 degrees as Shima, unable to contact Nishimura (and having made apparently no attempt to obtain a report from the *Shigure*), decided to retire 'to plan subsequent action'.

His force's contribution to the Battle of Surigao Strait was over.

Battle of Surigao Strait. Phase IV (25 October)

V Adm Shima, having signalled his intentions to Tokyo, recalled his destroyers and, at 0425, commenced his retirement. Perhaps finally influencing his decision was the appearance ahead of the *Mogami*, blazing and smoke-shrouded, apparently dead and abandoned. The *Nachi* was leading the *Ashigara* as the two cruisers manoeuvred to fire their torpedoes. Their turn was calculated to avoid the stricken *Mogami* but, too late, it was realized that the supposed derelict was still not only active but was under weigh at approaching ten knots. Aboard *Nachi* extreme rudder angle was applied but, at 28 knots, the big cruiser had considerable advance and a sideswipe was inevitable. For a few dangerous minutes after the impact, at 0430, the two ships were locked, bow to stern, until the *Nachi* was able to wrench herself free of the *Mogami's* fiery embrace.

The *Nachi* was now reduced to 18 knots and led her consort southward at this speed. To the amazement of those topside, they were slowly overhauled and joined by the valiant *Mogami*, whose engine room staff performed prodigies in working up their ruined ship to the same speed. The only other survivor, the still erratically-steering *Shigure*, also joined Shima's force.

A US navy patrol torpedo boat picks up survivors of a Japanese ship sunk in Surigao Strait. The PT boats carried out a dramatic torpedo attack on the night of 24–25 October. (Associated Press © EMPICS)

It was several minutes before it became apparent on Oldendorf's plotting tables that the remnants of the enemy's Southern Force were, in fact, retiring. The admiral immediately ordered off the left flank cruisers in pursuit, led by his own flagship, the *Louisville*. In company were all but two of Capt Smoot's destroyers. To be certain, Oldendorf then ordered the right flank cruisers to conform, and recommended to Kinkaid that a dawn air strike be mounted by Sprague's CVEs (although, as we have seen, Kurita's imminent and unscheduled appearance would give the little carriers other priorities).

Perhaps due to reaction and fatigue, Oldendorf's pursuit seemed half-hearted, begun at only 15 knots. None the less American radars first acquired the Japanese at about 0500. This was unexpected, and the reason rapidly became apparent, for Shima was again heading northward. The motive for this turnabout is not recorded, perhaps a growing realization that he might have supported his plucky subordinates a little better. Whatever the cause, this outburst of resolution did not last and he quickly resumed his retreat.

At 0520, in gathering daylight, Oldendorf gained sight of his quarry. Still 'burning like a city block', the unfortunate *Mogami* attracted the combined fire of Oldendorf's three leading cruisers. However, apparently apprehensive of Japanese torpedo expertise, the American admiral eschewed the opportunity to complete the Southern Force's annihilation. Even as the luckless *Mogami* began to absorb yet more punishment, Oldendorf hauled away to the north, probably assuming that Sprague's aircraft could complete the job. It was 0537.

Again spared, the *Mogami* was reduced to six knots and soon lost touch with the remainder of Shima's group. By 0600 she was again having to ward off the attentions of PT boats. Again, it was found that a hot and sustained fire was the most effective antidote to such minor irritants. At 0645, in the strengthening sunlight of a new day, *Mogami's* weary crew, with the help of a destroyer, fought off the last challenge. Now bereft of the cloak of darkness, the PT boats had again failed to make much impression in the teeth of a resolute defence.

Oldendorf, too, had revised thoughts about his premature retirement and, at 0617, again turned to the south. Half an hour later, he directed R Adm Robert W. Hayler, with the light cruisers *Denver* and *Columbia* and

HMAS *Australia* showing damaged sustained to her superstructure during the landings on Leyte. (NARA)

three destroyers, to finish off the enemy stragglers. They quickly over-hauled the destroyer *Asagumo*, which had lost much of her bow section to an earlier destroyer torpedo. Hopelessly out-gunned, the Japanese valiantly fought her after mounting until the waters closed over her at 0730.

Almost intuitively, Oldendorf again re-considered the position and, at 0730, recalled Hayler at the point where his force was poised to complete its designated task. Just two minutes later came the galvanizing news that Sprague's CVEs were in action with Kurita's heavy forces. For the moment, Shima's luck held as his pursuers, already short on fuel and ammunition, worked up to maximum speed in the opposite direction to assist in the crisis developing around Leyte Gulf.

MOPPING UP

The Closing Phases (25–27 October)

Subsequent to the major actions described above it will be apparent that, at some point during 25 October, no less than three Japanese admirals, Shima, Kurita and Ozawa, were in retreat and seeking to save as great a proportion of their defeated forces as possible. It remained the task of the Americans to capitalize on their disorder and to pick off the damaged and the vulnerable.

Chronologically, the first group to seek safety in retirement was the Southern Force, which turned about at 0425. As Oldendorf vacillated about further surface action to annihilate Shima, Sprague's CVEs, yet untroubled, took the initiative. In response to Oldendorf's recommendation to Kinkaid, they despatched an air strike at 0545. It was 0910 before this found the gravely damaged *Mogami*, as she exited the strait to enter the Mindanao Sea. Torpedoed by Avengers, she was finally brought to a halt. A destroyer took off her survivors and, at 1230, finished her off with a further torpedo.

The light cruiser *Abukuma*, the only recipient of a PT boat torpedo during the early hours, was unable to keep up with Shima. Falling out, she sought sanctuary in the small Mindanao port of Dapitan. Having completed emergency repairs, she sailed again on 27 October, only to be found and sunk off Negros Island by a considerable force of US Army bombers.

Once freed from the attentions of Kurita's Centre Group, Sprague's game little CVEs again attended to Oldendorf's earlier request with a valedictory strike against Shima, now at a considerable range. The aircraft found Shima, already deep into the Mindanao Sea, at about 1500 on the 25th, but were able only to damage a destroyer. Shima, having contributed nothing to the actions around Leyte Gulf, extricated himself with two heavy cruisers and five destroyers.

Following his hectic and undisciplined scrap with Thomas Sprague's CVEs off Samar, Kurita, after a considerable period of indecision, began his withdrawal by signal at 1236 on 25 October. Despite being hit by two long-range strikes, from McCain's TG 38.1 and from Taffy 1, the Centre Group suffered negligible further damage before it disappeared back into the San Bernardino Strait between 2100 and 2200. The destroyer *Nowake*, however, left behind to stand by the doomed *Chikuma*, was found and sunk about midnight by TF 34.5

By 0500 on 26 October Task Groups 38.1 and 38.2 were positioned to despatch further raids while Kurita was still in range. The fugitives were duly located at 0810 and were quickly attacked by a first strike, which had been aloft since 0600. During the forenoon two further strikes were despatched. As noted briefly above, the first casualty was the heavy cruiser *Kumano*. Already lacking her bows, she took a damaging bomb hit at about 0900. Capable of only five knots, the ship left the formation and survived the battle. Temporarily repaired, she was never to leave the Philippines, being finally sunk by carrier aircraft on 25 November.

Also hit in the first strike was the light cruiser *Noshiro*, which foundered near Panay nearly three hours later.

Land-based Army B-24s also gave Kurita a thorough shaking on the morning of the 26th yet, despite ambitious claims, scored no hits. Indeed, the only further 'kill' was that of the destroyer *Hayashimo* which, desperately low on fuel, had to divert to meet with a tanker. On the 27th she was caught by aircraft near Mindoro. Damaged, she had to be beached, where she was bombed to a wreck.

Thanks to his timely retirement Kurita, too, had preserved a goodly proportion of his force.

From about 0630 on 25 October Ozawa's Northern Force was headed in a generally northern direction, less a retirement than a continuation of its role in enticing Halsey's Third Fleet as far north as possible.

Although he had despatched TF 34 southward at 1115, Halsey held back a squadron of four cruisers with which to finish off Ozawa's stragglers. Under the command of R Adm Laurance T. DuBose, this was first in action at 1625, sinking the stricken *Chiyoda* by gunfire.

As dusk gathered, carrier-based reconnaissance aircraft located three Japanese destroyers. These were brought under fire by the cruisers at extreme range at about 1900 but DuBose was frustrated by the enemy manoeuvring boldly as if to launch torpedoes. Showing due deference, the American admiral sent off his own destroyers to deal with the Japanese. They were able to isolate and sink, by gunfire and torpedo, only the largest of the three enemy ships, the *Hatsuzuki*, which went down at about 2100.

These operations delayed DuBose sufficiently to allow Ozawa to retire with the remainder of his force. The American cruisers were, in any case, no match for Ozawa's surviving pair of hybrid battleships, while the Japanese were now well beyond the strike range of Mitscher's remaining carrier groups.

Ozawa's final loss was that of the light cruiser *Tama*. Already bomb-damaged, she was sunk by submarine torpedo at 2310 on 25 October.

In its sacrificial role, the Northern Force lost all its four carriers, together with a light cruiser and three destroyers. Nevertheless, Adm Ozawa, his mission successful, brought back his two battleships, another light cruiser and five destroyers.

USS *Pennsylvania* in an Advanced Base Sectional Dock (ABSD) which allowed US naval assets to be re-refitted or repaired in the battle theatre. (NARA)

A US SB2C Helldiver from USS *Essex* bombs Japanese carriers at Kure. (NARA)

CONCLUSION

An American Naval War College publication of 1936 noted that, in naval warfare, 'mistakes are normal, errors are usual; information is seldom complete, often inaccurate and frequently misleading'. This passage could have been written after the Battles for Leyte Gulf and with direct reference to them.

Between 23 and 26 October, the landings in the Philippines triggered a series of clashes that, together, constitute the greatest naval engagement of all time. It invites direct comparison with Jutland, where a British fleet with a three to two numerical advantage failed to materially defeat its German opponent. At Leyte, a similarly crude comparison gives the Allies (there were two Australian ships present) an advantage of nearly three to one. This, however, would be to ignore the fact that practically all the air power was vested in the American fleet, whose paper advantage was over-whelming. The final, and not altogether satisfactory, outcome resulted from a mix of incomplete and misinterpreted intelligence, unsound decisions and assumptions, and a distinct whiff of ego. Admirals, after all, are human.

Having predicted that Kurita's force would sortie from Lingga to attack Leyte and having correctly deduced the route that it would take, the Americans posted submarines with orders to report but not to attack. They reported but could not resist an opportunity. In depriving the Japanese of three heavy cruisers, they were drawn off station and failed to report either Nishimura or Shima. Further, the wreck of the stranded *Dace* was insufficiently destroyed, reportedly allowing the enemy subsequently to retrieve items yielding valuable intelligence.

Of the Japanese admirals, only Ozawa emerges with reputation intact. Nishimura and Shima had personal differences, preferring to follow orders to the letter rather than to employ common sense. Nishimura's courage is beyond dispute but, once he knew that Kurita's main thrust had been delayed, it was clearly suicidal for him not to also delay his arrival.

Kurita's own actions can be ascribed only to acute fatigue following nearly three days without sleep and having had two flagships sunk under him. Ozawa's coat-trailing had worked so well that Kurita had Kinkaid's light forces at his mercy, for all available Seventh Fleet heavy units had been committed to blocking Nishimura and Shima. Throughout the action off Samar, however, Kurita and his staff mistook CVEs for fleet carriers, and destroyers for cruisers, simple mis-identification which resulted first in his order for general chase and the consequent uncoordinated action. His subsequent retirement he never satisfactorily explained, alluding to having to intercept a further Third Fleet carrier group which, simply, was not true.

A final, and major contributory failing was Fukudome's inability to admit, and, reluctance to make clear, that his land-based air support had already been reduced to virtual impotence.

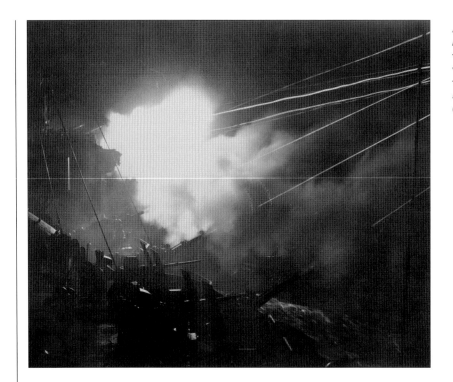

Halsey, who died in 1959, spent the rest of his life trying to justify his reasons for taking the Third Fleet north. His burning desire for fleet action to crown his career made him the perfect target for Ozawa's enticement strategy but, even allowing for the fact that he could not have known just how few aircraft his opponent had, he (Halsey) had sufficient strength both to cover the San Bernardino Strait and to annihilate Ozawa. The truth, unfortunately, was that to follow this correct procedure would have left him in his flagship *New Jersey*, awaiting the Centre Group rather than engaging the Northern Force, where he yearned to be. In various subsequent defences of his action he criticized divided command (a reasonable point but one which implicitly questioned the judgement of his superiors) and also the actions of Kinkaid.

Halsey and Kinkaid had been friends since Naval Academy days, but the former's assertion that his colleague had been somehow deficient in allowing his forces to be surprised by Kurita turned friendship to recrimination. Nevertheless, Kinkaid's blind acceptance that Halsey was covering the San Bernardino Strait was a grave error. However unlikely the alternative, it is a commander's duty to check.

Even Oldendorf, who oversaw a textbook victory in the Surigao Strait, showed later indecision, failing to take risks in order to pursue his beaten opponent to annihilation.

Human frailties and poor communication procedures contributed, therefore, to preventing a great victory becoming total victory. Following the Battle of the Philippine Sea in the preceding June, the Imperial Japanese Navy needed time to re-train. The Americans correctly denied it that time by obliging it to make a total commitment over Leyte. Although a considerable proportion of the Japanese surface fleet yet survived, it was never again able to seriously challenge American naval supremacy.

APPENDIX

WARSHIPS DESTROYED

IMPERIAL JAPANESE NAVY

Northern Force (V Adm Ozawa)

Name	Standard Displacement	Date Sunk
Zuikaku (CV)	25,675	25 October
Chitose (CVL)	11,190	25 October
Chiyoda (CVL)	11,190	25 October
Zuiho (CVL)	11,262	25 October
Tama (CL)	5,870	25 October
Akitsuki (DD)	2,701	25 October
Hatsuzuki (DD)	2,701	25 October

Centre Group (V Adm Kurita)

Name	Standard Displacement	Date Sunk
Musashi (BB)	64,170	24 October
Atago (CA)	13,160	23 October
Chikuma (CA)	11,215	25 October
Chokai (CA)	13,160	25 October
Maya (CA)	13,160	23 October
Suzuya (CA)	12,400	25 October
Noshiro (CL)	6,652	26 October
Fujinami (DD)	2,077	27 October
Hayashimo (DD)	2,077	26 October
Nowake (DD)	2,033	26 October

Southern Force, Van (V Adm Nishimura)

Name	Standard Displacement	Date Sunk
Fuso (BB)	34,700	25 October
Yamashiro (BB)	34,700	25 October
Mogami (CA)	12,400	25 October
Asagumo (DD)	1,961	25 October
Michishio (DD)	1,961	25 October
Yamagumo (DD)	1,961	25 October

Southern Force, Rear (V Adm Shima)

Name	Standard Displacement	Date Sunk
Abukuma (CL)	5,170	26 October
Shiranuhi (DD)	2,033	27 October
Wakaba (DD)	1,715	24 October

UNITED STATES NAVY

Third Fleet (Adm Halsey)

Name	Standard Displacement	Date Sunk
Princeton (CVL)	11,000	25 October

Seventh Fleet (V Adm Kinkaid)

Name	Standard Displacement	Date Sunk
Gambier Bay (CVE)	7,800	25 October
St Lo (CVE)	7,800	25 October
Hoel (DD)	2,050	25 October
Johnston (DD)	2,050	25 October
Eversole (DE)	1,350	29 October
Samuel B. Roberts (DE)	1,350	25 October

Abbreviations:
(BB) Battleship (CV) Fleet Carrier (CVL) Light Carrier (CVE) Escort Carrier (CA) Heavy Cruiser
(CL) Light Cruiser (DD) Destroyer (DE) Destroyer Escort

FURTHER READING

History books come in three broad categories. At the top is the broad-brush strategic viewpoint, giving reasons for an operation like Leyte Gulf and putting it in context in terms of objectives. Next come those dealing with the operation at a tactical level – how it was conducted, what happened next and the consequences. Included among these are the many reminiscences of senior commanders. At the bottom level are the personal stories, the first-hand accounts of those who were actually at the 'sharp end'.

Beginning at the top, and in order to grasp overall American strategy in the Pacific, a good starting point is *War Plan Orange – The US Strategy to Defeat Japan 1897–1945* by Edward S. Miller (US Naval Institute, Annapolis, Md., 1991), which shows how the United States anticipated the problem precisely and planned long-term and in detail to deal with it.

Now coming on 50 years old, but still the best account of Leyte Gulf and the reasons for it, is Volume XII of Samuel Eliot Morison's *History of US Naval Operations in World War II* (OUP, London,1958). Entitled simply *Leyte: June 1944–January 1945,* it remains an excellent account by an eyewitness historian. Being written so soon after the event, however, it lacks the background of Allied intelligence. This may be filled by such as John Prado's *Combined Fleet Decoded* (Random House, New York, 1995). Hardly bedtime reading but valuable.

Written 20 years later than Morison, and using some Japanese material, is Paul S. Dull's *A Battle History of the Imperial Japanese Navy (1941–1945)* (US Naval Institute,1978), which offers occasional differing perspectives.

For the military viewpoint of the assault and its follow-up, the official version is again hard to better. The series on *The US Army in WWII – The War in the Pacific* includes *Leyte – The Return to the Philippines* by M. Hamlin Cannon (Washington DC, 1982). Clearly written and with good maps.

Good insights into the various naval actions are afforded by the autobiographies and biographies of senior commanders. Fleet Admiral Ernest J. King, the CNO, is well covered by *Fleet Admiral King: A Naval Record* by Walter M. Whitehill (Eyre & Spottiswoode, London, 1953). An austere account of an austere personality.

The contradiction that was Halsey has been covered extensively, but Professor E.B. Potter's *Bull Halsey* (US Naval Institute, 1985) remains as good as any. It also makes an interesting counterpoint to *Nimitz* by the same author (1976), although history can never really explain Nimitz' extraordinary tolerance of his wayward subordinate's actions.

At one command level down, good insights into the operational philosophy of the Fast Carrier Force can be gained from *The Magnificent Mitscher* by Theodore Taylor (Norton, New York, 1954) and from Frederick C. Sherman's *Combat Command* (Dutton, New York, 1950). Sherman commanded one of Mitscher's carrier task groups and his recollections were still fresh.

Input into the Leyte Gulf actions by the Submarine Commands was of variable quality, but significant. Clay Blair's *Silent Victory* (Lippincott, Philadelphia and New York, 1975) remains a magnificent and exhaustive study of US underwater operations which, given time, and taken to their logical conclusion, might simply have starved Japan into submission. But that is another story.

Good reading!

Bernard Ireland. 2005

INDEX